COMMUNITIES OF YOUTH

Communities of Youth

Cultural practice and informal learning

STEVEN MILES, AXEL POHL, BARBARA STAUBER,
ANDREAS WALTHER, RUI MANUEL BARGIELA BANHA
AND MARIA DO CARMO GOMES

ASHGATE

Published by
Ashgate Publishing Limited
Gower House
Croft Road
Aldershot
Hants GU11 3HR
England

Ashgate Publishing Company
131 Main Street
Burlington, VT 05401-5600 USA

Ashgate website: http://www.ashgate.com

British Library Cataloguing in Publication Data
Communities of youth
    1.Youth - Europe 2.Youth - Education (Continuing education)
    - Europe 3.School-to-work transition - Europe
    I.Miles, Steven
    305.2'35'094

Library of Congress Cataloging-in-Publication Data
Communities of youth / Steven Miles ...[et.al.].
        p. cm.
    Includes bibliographical references and index.
    ISBN-0-7546-1976-1 (alk paper)
    1. Youth--Europe. 2. School-to-work transition--Europe. 3. Performing arts and youth--Europe. 4. Active learning--Europe. I. Miles, Steven.

HQ799.E9 C65 2002
305.235'094--dc21

                                                            2002066705

ISBN 0 7546 1976 1

Printed and bound in Great Britain by Antony Rowe Ltd, Chippenham, Wiltshire

Contents

List of Tables   *vi*
Preface   *vii*

1   Introduction   1

2   Youth Transitions   7

3   Researching Communities of Youth: Some thoughts on
    methodology   27

4   Case Studies   37

5   'Catching the Trapeze in the Learning Society': The Evaluation of
    Case Studies   97

6   Conclusions   121

Bibliography   *131*
Index   *139*

List of Tables

Table 2.1   Change of status of young people in Germany,
             Portugal, the United Kingdom and in the European
             Union between 1987 (1990) and 1995 (per cent) 11
Table 5.1   Dimensions of formality in JUST, Hope Street and
             Chapitô 109
Table 5.2   Starting positions, challenges and current positions
             of the three study cases 112

Preface

'Communities of Youth' is concerned with addressing the challenges young women and men face as regards the changing nature of youth as a life stage. High youth unemployment rates and disengagement from post-compulsory education are just two examples of the structural changes young people are having to cope with in what has often been described as a 'risk' society. Despite these changes Western countries continue to develop social policies based on a conception of 'youth' as a relatively straightforward transitional phase in people's lives. This book argues that the time has come to adopt a more radical approach to what and how young men and women learn and how learning relates to young people's transitions. In this context, the book discusses the results of a comparative European research project which sought to link young people's actual experience of 'youth training' to the development of their lifestyles in community settings. 'Communities of Youth' is particularly concerned with addressing the value of performing arts as a source for informal learning which encourages young people to 'find themselves' and to develop a sense of self-belief that they cannot apparently achieve through more traditional training regimes.

'Communities of Youth' will provide academics and students in the fields of sociology, community work and education with a considered and theoretically informed examination of aspects of young people's experience of training in an applied context. It will therefore be of particular interest to practitioners in the field of youth work and youth training.

We thank the European Commission's DG Education and Culture who funded parts of the research this book under their programme 'Youth for Europe'. We are grateful to all the staff members at Hope Street Ltd. (Liverpool), Chapitô (Lisbon), and Gemeinschaftszentrum Jungbusch (Mannheim) for sharing their time and their knowledge of young people's lives with us. Above all, we wish to thank all the young women and men in Lisbon, in Liverpool and in Mannheim who gave us an insight into the creative and inventive nature of their transitions. It is thanks to them that the field work for this research was both an intellectually fruitful and a thoroughly enjoyable experience.

Chapter 1

Introduction

This book is concerned with the exploration of non-conventional means of empowering young people in their transitions to work and adulthood. Biographical transitions are normally related to status passages between different phases of the life-course. As such they refer to learning: the acquisition of knowledge and skills inherent to the demands of the life-phase to come. Institutionalized forms of organizing this kind of learning mainly focus on the skills and qualifications young people need. But equally important to the process of learning is the development of competencies necessary for coping with these demands in a subjectively meaningful and individually viable way. This issue represents a key focus of this book.

Recent research on transitional systems in Europe (EGRIS, 2001; Walther *et al.*, 2002) has shown that the structures of formal education and training have failed in preparing a considerable percentage of young people appropriately for the demands associated with entering the labour market and constructing their own biographies in a way which makes sense for them. First, educational structures cannot avoid, and sometimes re-produce or even re-inforce, inequalities in the qualifications starting postions of young people. This means restricted options for individual choice and high risks of social exclusion for those with the lowest qualifications (Kieselbach *et al.*, 2001). Secondly, many schools and training organizations obviously have lost touch with the needs of a changing economy and a changing workforce. They seem to be simply not in tune with changing labour market needs, with young people's life plans nor with the requirements of coping with the everyday life of transitions which follow less and less linear and predictable routes. This dilemma is due to the constraints of the societal organization of learning in general, which, in one way or the other, puts a strong emphasis on selection. It is very difficult, if not impossible, to create a balance between the principles of selection and integration. Meanwhile, it is also true to say that economic and social demands alter so rapidly that it is equally difficult to foresee and plan learning needs in advance. In contrast, it has become obvious that formal education and training have ceased to be a reliable defence against unemployment and against increasingly precarious futures. Many young people find themselves in a situation in which they are forced to deal with the uncertainties caused by so-called flexible labour markets and globalized economies. In these circumstances the transition itself is undermined. It is certainly not the case that such young people are not capable enough to cope with the demands of a changing world. Rather, our suggestion here is that the skills and knowledge they are offered by mainstream education and training are not giving them the tools they need to survive and to prosper.

Many young people react to these circumstances by withdrawing from formal education and training. They therefore become labelled as 'disadvantaged', and any problems they have tend to be ascribed to individual deficiencies rather than to be regarded as deficiencies of the system as a whole. Young people therefore inevitably feel stigmatized and pressurized into lowering their aspirations towards those jobs and training schemes available to them, however inappropriate they may be. Feeling demotivated they do not expect any subjectively meaningful support from public institutions in general and from agencies such as vocational counselling, and the careers and employment services.

This monograph seeks to question the universal validity of formal qualifications and formally acquired skills and calls for investment in alternative forms of training and education which provide young people with the skills they actually need. The book is based upon the findings of a European research project under the title of 'Secondary learning effects of community arts' funded by the European Commission's programme 'Youth for Europe' from 1997 to 2000. With the notion of 'secondary learning effects', we tried to express our particular interest in the more implicit learning processes which do occur in education and training programmes for young men and women rather beyond their official curriculum: by developing a drama piece or a music show, for example (which may be the direct purpose of a project), arrangements with the other group members have to be made, individuals have to rehearse with and in front of the group and in these circumstances self-confidence may be enhanced. However, we no longer wish to be beholding to the label 'secondary' learning effects, because it implies that such learning effects are somehow inferior to 'primary' learning effects. Our suggestion is that they are in fact equally important and perhaps more so than the more explicit skills that young people acquire in these contexts. The central objective of this research was therefore to assess the experiential effect of performance in the following semi-formal settings: community arts, cultural youth work, and in circus and theatre schools. We hope to be able to illustrate the value of indirect learning as a means of coping with transitions into work and adulthood.

Our cross-cultural research was carried out in three European cities – Liverpool (United Kingdom), Lisbon (Portugal) and Mannheim (Germany) – and it deals with experiences of young men and women in the context of performing arts: drama and acting, music and dance. In Liverpool Hope Street Ltd. gives unemployed young people the opportunity to express themselves in music and drama and to acquire workshop skills in the context of community arts projects conducted with children, youngsters, and elderly or disabled people. In Lisbon Chapitô is a professional school offering courses and recognized qualifications in the area of circus skills. In Mannheim the community centre JUST ('Youth in the Neighbourhood') serves young people from migrant backgrounds and uses drama and music as a means of preventive youth work.

Why performing arts? Firstly, we start from the assumption that young people have a high subjective interest in performing which, certainly at an informal level, plays a key role in the construction of youth cultural lifestyles and identities. Secondly, we contend that young people develop knowledge and skills in these aspects of their lives. Thirdly, we argue that such competencies are in actual fact highly appropriate given the changing demands of the labour market and the changing shape of individual biographies. They are in turn in line with what has been identified as modern key competencies: creativity, networking and group skills, learning to learn, improvization and flexibility. And they potentially deliver a very important resource for transition processes: motivation. In addition, the performing arts in particular, potentially provide equally invaluable and yet undervalued qualities such as self-confidence, personal standing, more open attitudes to fellow human beings and more flexible attitudes towards gender relations.

The argument that alternative forms of learning are needed to respond to the demands of changing biographies in late modern youth has several consequences: Vocational training and education can no longer be reduced to the acquisition of job-related skills, but have to be seen in the context of the increasing need of young people to make sense of their youth biographies which is no longer supplied by the modern promise of 'learn now and profit later'. With the attempt to broaden the access of young people to socially recognized forms of learning, this research is located in the context of the discourse on lifelong learning and the building of a 'learning society'. In general this means that social change requires a fundamental restructuring of the societal organization of learning. The role of learning institutions in individuals lives and vice versa needs to be reconsidered. There is a danger that debates concerning lifelong learning are nothing more than rhetorical. Many authors have indeed underlined the fact that such a discourse reflects a status quo in which segmented learning opportunities persist (Stauber and Walther, 1999; Coffield, 1999a). The danger is that lifelong learning becomes little more than a 'container' in which the unemployed are temporarily 'deposited'. The unemployed are likely to be de-motivated and under-qualified in these conditions. It is therefore absolutely crucial to identify and encourage more 'proactive' approaches to 'training for jobs' and to invest in 'innovative' 'learning for change' (Manninen, 1998) in which individuals have an active say in their own training experience. The interest in identifying more informal learning settings and to assess the potential of such settings is motivated by this critical approach to lifelong learning. A necessary prerequisite of a learning society which is currently a long way from being a reality, can therefore be said to be the empowerment of informal spaces and contexts in which learning is embedded in social and cultural practice. The debate as to how informal learning can be strengthened under conditions of late modernity is one of the major challenges to both educationalists and youth researchers. Thus, the various levels of organizations concerned need to foster more open learning processes. Crucially, they also need to be prepared to be brave enough to accept uncertain, and often unmeasurable, learning outcomes. To support this paradigm shift from a teaching curriculum to a learning-based curriculum is one of the objectives of this publication. From a youth research perspective we therefore will link the issue of how learning could be organized along the life-course closely to the issue of re-thinking the concept of youth transitions.

The book is organized in five chapters. Chapter 2 offers a theoretical view on the changes in young people's transitions. It contends that youth transitions should be conceptualized not merely as prolonged but also as de-standardized in nature. In other words, they offer a dizzying array of options and opportunities as well as risks, depending on individual access to resources and spaces. However, in order to avoid constructing a stereotypical image of young people as mere victims of structural conditions the chapter also deals with the strategies which young men and women adopt in order to cope with transitions and in order to shape their own lives. At the end of this chapter we consider how far performing arts represent an appropriate means of empowering young people in these uncertain times.

Chapter 3 describes the methodological design and procedure of the research and focuses on the following main dimensions: the analysis of organizations and policies which we investigated by expert interviews, document analysis and participatory observation, the analysis of young people's experiences and orientations by focus group interviews and biographic interviews, and the evaluation of these findings through an intercultural perspective.

In Chapter 4 the three case studies are presented. These presentations start from a description of the respective national transition systems representing the institutional and socio-economic context of the analyzed projects. We then discuss the organizational structure, history and overall objectives of the three projects. The operationalization of these objectives into pedagogical concepts and methods is analyzed according to interviews with project workers. Then this 'official' perspective is compared and contrasted with young people's own experiences of each project. These are related to their experiences and expectations prior to the project as well as to their future orientations. An integral part of these presentations is the analytical description of an actual performance.

In Chapter 5 the above case studies are evaluated with regard to three key dimensions: their relation to and relevance for the transitions and lives of the young people involved; the learning processes and the effects and impact of such processes and the prerequisites which are necessary for these processes to be effective. The findings will be related to and interpreted by means of theoretical concepts such as identity, motivation and self-confidence, informal learning and empowerment, community and institutionalization.

In Chapter 6 we present conclusions regarding the future of indirect learning and its impact on youth transitions with particular reference to the performing arts. We also consider the implications of this relationship for the nature of youth research in this area. By doing so we intend to provide a foundation upon which future research can develop. Our suggestion is that young people are too often constrained by training that fails to engage with young people's lifestyles and with the meanings they invest in their everyday lives. In short, we call for an investment in indirect learning which is itself remarkable for the way in which how it creates an environment in which young people are the authors of their own training and in which they begin to have a direct say in their own futures.

Chapter 2

Youth Transitions

This chapter will deal with the increasing complexity and ambivalence of transitions between youth and adulthood which has been a recurring feature of recent research concerned with the prolongation of the youth phase (Cavalli and Galland, 1995). In a rapidly changing world the transition into adulthood is not a straightforward process. The transition is itself constituted by a whole spectrum of transitions taking place in various contexts, all of which follow their own rules, whilst create their own sense of normality. In addition, such transitions are located in their own time and space; challenging individuals to negotiate their own paths. However, in public discourses as well as in research, the transition from youth to adulthood is often reduced to the transition between school and work (see Cohen and Ainley, 2000). But it is more than this approach may suggest. In particular, these transitions are ambivalent insofar as they are characterized at one and the same time by cultural autonomy *and* prolonged dependency, notably with regard to housing and economic dependency. In what follows we will outline the structural demands of these new transitions, but instead of leaving our analysis there (as much youth research tends to do) we will go on to address the *active* ways in which young people relate to structural constraints on their lives.

As a first step we will have a closer look at the nature of re-structured youth transitions. We will try to identify the main risks and demands that emerge from these structural contexts. *Secondly,* we will focus on the solutions and strategies young men and women develop themselves. We are especially interested in how young women and men cope with complex and contradictory demands and at the same time try to do this in a *meaningful* way. *Thirdly,* we will outline what prerequisites young people need for making subjectively satisfying and meaningful solutions: what do they need as regards resources, competencies and learning environments? We will then conclude this section by presenting a hypothesis concerned with how far performing arts represent an appropriate means to empower young people in coping with the sorts of transitional demands under discussion.

The de-standardization and fragmentation of transitions

Various types of transitions occur in young people's lives, all of which share the objectives of an individual balancing subjective aspirations within structural constraints: the transition to work, the transition to independence (from the family), the transition towards responsible and fulfilling partnership and sexuality, the transition towards an individual lifestyle, and the transition towards citizenship. A horizontal objective, integral to all biographic transitions, is the construction of sexual and gender identity: what does it mean to become a man or woman?

The above transitions interact, often in a contradictory fashion, and the individual has to navigate and to negotiate them the best he or she can, notably in the context of family and intergenerational relationships, sexual and gender relations, education and training, the labour market, locally and regionally, as well as in cultural contexts and most importantly, in the context of youth cultures. Resources for negotiation and navigation differ significantly according to gender, social backgrounds and ethnic and cultural origins. From a theoretical point of view it is therefore important, notably in the context of post-modernism, that lines of social segmentation are regarded in relation to gender and ethnicity, social background and age, for instance (Bradley, 1996). Young people's biographies seem to be characterized, above all, by paradox. Young people have to cope with a situation in which they are both young and adult at the same time, but in different life contexts, or in which they are none of the above. They can indeed be said to live in a form of transitional purgatory. Many young people simply feel that they do not fit in. For instance, in their origin-culture young Turkish females in Germany are regarded as adults much earlier than their German friends. In the dominant culture in which they live, however, they are treated as young people without any rights. This represents a source of considerable confusion and uncertainty. As Bauman (1995) argues this can be interpreted as a consequence of the *fragmentation* of individual biographies and social life (Bauman, 1995); a feature of contemporary life which is apparently especially pertinent to the everyday experiences of young people who have often been described as barometers of social change (Jones and Wallace, 1992).

Perhaps the most important characteristics of youth transitions is that young people are obliged to develop appropriate and complimentary coping strategies which are sophisticated enough to cope with the contradictory nature of their own experiences:

'In other words, young people's lives seem to bounce back and forth like a yo-yo. These oscillatory and reversible movements suggest that what has happened is the *yo-yo-isation* of the transition to adulthood. As if young people had gone to live in the skies and migrated **like birds**.' (Pais, 2000: pp. 220).

Transitions and life courses in general lose their linearity: they have no clear beginning and no clear ending any more, their borders are getting more and more hazy. The very legitimacy of notions of 'youth' and 'adult-hood' have been undermined inasmuch as such transitions overlap with and undermine the life-phases we would traditionally associate with youth, adulthood and old age. Transitions no longer appear to represent secure and defined status passages. These status passages are no longer clear cut and are often, in fact, reversed. Routes towards independence often have to be rejected because of unemployment, inappropriate educational choices or broken relationships (Walther *et al.*, 1999).

Biographies and transitions *diversify* and *pluralize*. The linear and se-cure status passage model of 'youth' is superseded by a fragmented and reversible model and can therefore be conceptualized as a process of *de-standardization*. In order to avoid the limitations associated with the de-scription of an overly rigidly youth phase, we will re-cycle the metaphor of the 'yo-yo' (Pais, 1996, Peters and Bois-Reymond, 1996), in doing so we intend to highlight the particular character of de-standardized transitions. Such 'yo-yoing' is a symptom of general processes of modernization which dissolve institutionalized assumptions of normality such as 'regular work', 'family', 'male and female life courses', which are themselves less and less useful as reliable points of reference for young people in the process of transition and biography construction. The promise of guaranteed stable occupations given by educational and training have, in recent years, proved to be unrealistic, at least for a large proportion of young people whose so-cial situation pre-structures the resources and opportunities they have available to them. Young people therefore appear to be experiencing 'old' trajectories of inequality alongside 'new' risks and opportunities. Some-times a lack of social resources may provoke the (apparent) 'falling back' into traditional gender role models or, alternatively, nourish the wish to live a 'normal' life which is still shared by a majority of young people. Young people endow the insecurities and possibilities associated with transitions with their own meanings (Allatt and Yeandle, 1992; du Bois-Reymond, 1998; Walther, 2000). As a result new conventions may emerge: young people may actually not expect a secure job and as such a perilous route into adulthood is normalized.

Risks and Demands in the Context of School-to-Work-Transitions

Transitions between school and work have for a long time been subject of both research and politics. The (reductive) concentration on this part of the transition derives from the constitution of modern societies as labour societies in which social integration largely depends on gainful employment. In contrast to the relatively smooth transitions associated with the Fordist era the contraction of labour markets since the 1970s and 1980s has exposed young people to risks of marginalization. In this respect four parallel developments can be identified:

- the pressure on European labour markets caused by processes of technological rationalization, neo-liberal shareholder value-structures and intensified global competition;
- the increased labour market participation of women due to the need of independent sources of income and cultural emancipation;
- the structure of labour markets and welfare systems which are constructed as a means of protecting adult male breadwinners rather than for young people entering the labour market;
- the historical mismatch between competencies and qualifications provided by the education and training systems and the labour market caused by the modernization of production and the shift from the manufacturing to the service economy (Reich, 1993).

In Europe, the effects of these trends have been visible by dramatically rising rates of youth unemployment. In most countries young people represent the largest age group of unemployed people. From a European point of view, however, we find remarkable differences: youth unemployment varies between 4 per cent in Austria and as much as 40 per cent in Spain. The picture diversifies even more if one looks at the social composition of unemployment. Whereas in some Southern European countries the rates for young women are much higher than for men (e.g. Eurostat, 2000) we find the opposite in Great Britain (Roberts, 1995). These differences are influenced by general labour market performance in the respective countries, cultural patterns (e.g. regarding female employment), and by the actual constitution of particular transition systems. In Germany, for instance, youth unemployment has always been lower than the total unemployment rate because the dual apprenticeship system of employment training and education at school integrated a high percentage of young men and women in transition. In Southern Europe, and also in Great Britain until the late 1970s, school leavers entered the labour market directly and were trained on the job. Since the end of full employment the youth labour market has been most affected by re-structuring (Pugliese, 1993; Roberts, 1995).

Table 2.1 Change of status of young people in Germany, Portugal, the United Kingdom and in the European Union between 1987 (1990) and 1995 (per cent)

	Germany		Portugal		United Kingdom		European Union	
	Male	*Fem.*	*Male*	*Fem.*	*Male*	*Fem.*	*Male*	*Fem.*
Active								
1987	39.0	38.0	63.0	48.0	56.0	50.0	47.0	41.0
1995	33.0	32.0	41.0	33.0	50.0	43.0	38.0	33.0
Unemployed								
1990	4.3	4.7	8.4	11.9	11.9	9.6	13.9	17.6
1995	8.9	8.7	15.1	18.5	18.0	13.3	20.1	23.2
In education or training								
1987	59.0	55.0	33.0	38.0	42.0	36.0	50.0	48.0
1995	65.0	61.0	55.0	60.0	47.0	44.0	58.0	58.0

Source: European Commission, 1997a; 1997b.

Despite structural differences the inherent difficulties in entering the labour market have lead to an increase in educational participation across Europe. Not only have individuals stayed longer at school in order to expand their qualification profile, but governments have also actively introduced policies to make young people more 'employable' (European Commission, 1997c). A major policy priority has focused on the implementation and/or development of vocational training systems, either as a part of the public school system or in different models of company-based apprenticeship systems. Alongside these 'mainstream' training opportunities, various schemes for 'disadvantaged' young people have been designed. These policies start from the assumption that a certain percentage of young people fail in entering regular training and employment due to individual deficiencies which have to be compensated in order that such young people are 'mature' or 'prepared' enough for participation in regular training programmes. However, the status of such schemes varies nationally as there are also examples (e.g. Italy, United Kingdom) in which participation in pre-vocational schemes leads to accredited partial qualifications which can be combined with further education or training (European Commission, 1997b).

European research has shown that integrative policies underlie institutional assumptions of normality (e.g. the legitimacy of individual aspirations, individual ascriptions of failure etc.) which, combined with their bureaucratic application, may actually lead to 'misleading trajectories' (EGRIS, 2001). As a result, the criteria of eligibility for participation may have a too narrow (or too wide) definition of the target group. This leads to the exclusion of individuals. Schemes aimed at the compensation of individual deficiencies may well therefore have a negative impact insofar as they may actually encourage stigmatization. They may well restrict individuals liberty of choice; whilst providing measures which apparently do little more than contain the superfluous labour force in order to 'clean' or 'massage' the unemployment statistics. Such policies often reproduce discourses of full employment, standard work arrangements and standard biographies which are simply unrealistic on a political, economic and a personal level. The transitional systems in which young people operate are therefore dominated by a series off in-built assumptions to which young people have to adapt. Otherwise they risk having to survive without any public support.

For young women and men the main new demands are to orientate themselves and to cope with the risk of personal failure. As such, most young people, should they have the opportunity, actively try to *postpone* their entrance into the labour market. This might involve continuing school education, the pursuit of alternative educational tracks or taking on additional forms of study or training courses. The postponement of labour market entrance depends, however, on important prerequisites. Such a postponement is simply not possible for those who do not have the necessary qualifications; for those who are lacking family support; or for those coming from a traditional background which discourages individual choice-making. In addition, young people may not have access to welfare provision, either because such provision is non-existent or because, as individuals, they are ineligible. There is a considerable danger of young people pursuing inflexible transitions, by for instance, becoming over-specialized and focused on a specific career path which may be too competitive to provide a realistic possibility of a secure future. Young people may also be forced to widen their geographical horizons. In addition they are often forced to seriously consider how to best balance family obligations against personal ones. Meeting these demands requires social, financial and educational resources which are simply not available to many young people. There are major variations in terms of the resources young people can call upon in order to cope with the demands of risky transitions which cannot be dealt with as straightforwardly as may have been the case in the past. The danger here is that a reasonably hassle-free transition may be taken for granted both institutionally and by the more informal support mechanisms called upon by young people, when the demands placed on young people are in actual fact very different to what they may have been previously, in terms of parental experience, for example.

A particular concern is that in the above circumstances young people are liable to be de-motivated. Being realistic about his or her employment potential may result in young people lowering their aspirations in advance. This was confirmed by Shell's (2000) study of young German women who, in the older cohorts, apparently start to anticipate difficulties in reconciling professional life and motherhood and as such lower their aspirations as regards training and work. Many young people with limited qualifications may therefore take anything they can get. A coping strategy might therefore involve shifting one's personal aspirations and expectations to other areas of life and by doing so replacing a subjective professional orientation with a mere 'job orientation'. For instance, a young person may aspire to work as a bar-person in a trendy bar or club. The ambiguity of such processes of adaptation is clear: it either may work out as the (only) appropriate way to preserve one's self-motivation, dignity and self-confidence. Alternatively, it may initiate a process of disintegration and/or marginalization.

A key phrase here is that of 'individualization'. Economic and social change is such that failure in the transition to work has become a general risk which has to be dealt with on an individual basis. This problem is sustained by institutions which perceive young people as 'carriers' of deficiencies which 'cause' such problems. Getting used to a system in which young people are rarely respected and in which they are more often than not perceived to be troublesome will encourage a set of circumstances in which the individual conceives of counselling agencies or training opportunities in a negative light. In contrast, young people actually often feel pressured to accept specific options in order not to lose social benefits (as is the case in United Kingdom), in order not to miss opportunities to earn money (which is a main topic for young people in Portugal) or in order not to fail the main entrance doors towards 'normal' work (which is the case in Germany). More generally, the opportunities available to young people simply do not 'speak' to their everyday lives. The danger, therefore, is that a situation is created in which young people are obliged to accept the options on offer or their benefits will be cut.

The context of family and generation relationships

Families play an especially important role as arbiters of the transition process in general, but more specifically as part of the transition from the family of origin to an independent life. Under conditions of late modernity transitions are related to and/or take place in the context of the family which in recent years has become increasingly diverse. All over Europe young people are staying at home longer. But despite the continuing reliance of young people on the family of origin there are big differences between different contexts in Europe on the character of such a reliance. Therefore 'staying longer at home' means a very different thing to young people all over Europe:

- In southern Europe (Italy, Portugal, Spain, and Greece) the convention is to stay at home until the individual starts his or her own family; this is enforced by a lack of welfare provision for young people which serves to reproduce a culture of familism.
- In northern Europe (Great Britain, Netherlands and the Scandinavian countries) the convention (at least for working class young people) is to move out from the parent's home at 16 or 18 at the point at which young people would aspire to enter the labour market. Decreasing access to labour market opportunities are, however, likely to increase young people's economic dependence on their family.
- In some other countries with a corporatist welfare regime such as Germany, the situation falls somewhere in between. Culturally, transitions are closely associated with autonomous housing, which in practice means leaving one's parents home. However, welfare provisions are conditioned by prior contributions to social insurance, i.e. regular employment. Individual access to social assistance is restricted until the age of 27.

Staying longer at the family home is often a 'necessary evil' as far as many young people are concerned. Meanwhile, many commentators have identified significant gender differences in this context (du Bois-Reymond, 1995; Lüscher, 1997). Young men and young women living in their parents' home are likely to take on different responsibilities in the family home, leading in general to a clearer domestic role for young women. As such, young women's subjective experience of family life mean that they are more liable to internalize domestic and caring responsibilities. In the case of divorce, for instance, the role of children may well vary, and in most cases, it is the daughter, who is expected to give practical support as regards household and child-care but also on an emotional and psychological level. Young women often become socio-psychological clearing institutions for their single parents (Stauber, 1999; Holland, 1990). Young people may often, therefore, find themselves within the boundaries of the family. On the other hand, the suffocating nature of domestic responsibility has resulted in young females leaving the parental home earlier than their male counterparts who have much more freedom and personal space at home.

In considering the above discussion there is a considerable need to re-conceptualize intergenerational relationships at both a societal and an individual level. Above all, young people should not be assumed to be, or portrayed as autonomous agents. Despite the apparent freedoms of a so-called risk society and the ideological aspirations of an individualized society they are still very much dependant upon their parents. In these circumstances young people's aspirations for autonomy remain important. But today processes of acquiring personal and social autonomy no longer develop in a linear fashion from total dependence to total independence – the latter amounting to a rather ideological male notion which ignores the general dependency of reproductive work and care. Today biographies switch between dependency and autonomy within what we have called yo-yo-movements. Young adults may achieve legal or civic autonomy, but still remain economically dependent on the family; they may move out of the family home only to return after a failed relationship or are economically forced to return due to unemployment. Likewise they may become economically independent, but still depend on their family in terms of emotional support. Therefore, young people more and more have to invent strategies how to deal with *semi-dependence* (see also Van de Velde 2001).

The context of gender relationships and sexuality

As we hinted above, transitions are differentiated according to gender. Particular social structures reproduce segmentation and hierarchies between men and women either in institutionalized contexts such as in school, labour market and welfare system, but also in non-institutional contexts in terms of peer and family relationships for instance (West and Zimmerman, 1987). But beyond this, transitions are inherently concerned with how to live as a man or a woman. This constitutes more than simply constructing a gendered identity. Questions of gender impinge upon all aspects of identity. The process of becoming a man or a woman is actually often influenced by a limited variety of images. Young people have few 'living examples' or role models to call upon as adequate points of reference. Those images that are available, notably through the media, tend to be one-dimensional and unrealistic. As far as young females are concerned, they appear to lie at two extremes: between domesticity at one end and 'girl power' at the other. In these circumstances there is a danger that traditional gender roles are maintained and that young people are not exposed to the broader range of possibilities, which in itself is an important aspect of a successful transition

(Böhnisch and Winter, 1993; Leccardi, 1996; Peters and du Bois-Reymond, 1996; du Bois-Reymond, 1998; Stauber, 1999). The problem here is that the labour market and public institutions in general are still based on a traditional gender-specific standard biography. On the other hand the pressures on young people are significant. There are significant demands on young women and men alike to overcome gender hierarchies in school-to-work-transitions, and yet in reality there is very little chance that such autonomy will be realized. As far as sexuality is concerned, for instance, genuine questions remain taboo in an atmosphere in which young women *have* to appear sexually sophisticated. And yet teenage pregnancy remains a major problem throughout Europe. Meanwhile, young men are mostly concerned with the reconciliation of different, even contradictory demands: to fulfil the role of the 'new man', whilst simultaneously fitting in with traditional patterns of masculinity (for example among their male peers). The development of gender identity in the sense of becoming a 'right' (or normal) man or woman is getting more and more complex for both males and females.

Demands in the context of migration and ethnic minorities

Another important influence on the construction of many young people's identities is migration and ethnicity. Young people from migrant or minority backgrounds have particular difficulties in fitting in with the dominant culture. In contrast to the representatives of the dominant culture who *may* interact with other cultures if and when they want to, representatives of migrant and minority cultures are constantly having to tackle the dominant culture and to cope with all-day racism (see Rommelspacher, 1992). This racism is also inbuilt in transitional systems – in structures as well as in behaviours and interactions with institutional representatives, with projects, with employers. Of special concern to young migrants is the permanent negotiation that goes on between the culture of origin and the culture of present stay – this negotiation of course is very different for a young Turkish guy living in Germany in the so-called 'third-generation' (with his grandfather representing the first generation of working migrants) compared to young people in Portugal or the United Kingdom stemming from a post-colonialist-background, or young people from recently migrated refugee families. This negotiation between cultures also gives high importance to intergenerational relationships. Besides all questions concerning school-to-work-transitions young people from **migrant backgrounds** therefore are **additionally concerned with the legal status** (in the context of migration); the future perspectives of the family (between staying in the immigration

country and returning to the country of origin; between orientating towards
the dominant culture or to cling to diasporic contexts); low school qualifications (due to language problems and lack of family support), and by the
ethnic segmentation of the labour market and training system (due to discrimi-
natory recruitment practices by both employers and vocational guidance).
The pressures on young migrants are such that the problems associated
with conventional transitions are magnified.

Demands deriving from youth cultural contexts

It might well be argued that young people perceive youth cultural contexts
they are involved in as the most important aspects of their everyday lives.
Young people's lifestyles represent an important way of establishing their
own social spaces and a sense of belonging.

> 'First, there is the simple selection of pre-existing items that can most easily
> be measured as consumption patterns. Next, tastes (and distastes) form a
> structure of habitus and attitudes. Finally, stylization refers to the process of
> active style production where values, meanings and artefacts are connected.
> These three dimensions of the way people orient themselves towards
> subcultures, genres or cultural arenas constitute a third way to discern
> vertical levels of lifestyles. Other levels and dimensions may also be
> constructed, pointing at the highly complex and flexible character of the
> lifestyle concept.' (Fornäs, 1995, p. 109).

In the above context it is important to consider how far biographical perspectives and transition decisions depend on criteria emerging from peer
relationships and lifestyles. Peer relationships are particularly important
given the ambiguities of 'fitting in and sticking out' (Miles *et al.*, 1998).
Fashion and leisure are not trivial activities but provide an important context in which young people make key decisions about their futures. The
demands on young people which arise from youth cultural involvement are
twofold: they have to orientate themselves in the landscape of lifestyles that
surround them, creating and occupying a niche they consider to be integrative as well as individual. In this sense youth lifestyles provide an arena
within which young people can at least attempt to assert their own agency.
This agency is a reflection of young people's broader relationship with social structures and the transition process in general (Miles, 2000).

All the above aspects of the transition process are significant. They are
also mutually dependant. They interact with each other, they have to be
coped with simultaneously, despite often contradicting each another, thus
making transitions ever more problematic for young people. The relation-

ships between these various domains are not necessarily synchronized which can, in itself, lead to frictions and asymmetry. For example, there may be considerable demands on young people to consume in particular ways, and yet such demands may conflict with the resources provided by the parental support upon which young people are so dependant.

These aspects of re-structuring transitions can be summarized as *de-standardization* in the sense that transitions are less and less predictable and increasingly risky in nature. At the same time however, de-standardization and individualization do not mean that individual transitions are only subject to individual decisions and agency. It is still undoubtedly the case that 'transitions are constituted by trajectories, and transitions are embedded in trajectories' (Hagestad, 1991, p. 23). In other words, young people's access to spaces of action and resources are still structured by processes of social reproduction. This has been conceptualized as 'structured individualization' (Evans and Heinz, 1994; Roberts *et al.*, 1994). Apart from 'inherited' capital however, in the course of their transitions, young women and men increasingly depend on institutions of welfare and education. Due to the difficulties facing them at the stage when they might expect to enter the labour market they are forced to participate in training and employment schemes, to use information and guidance facilities or to claim social benefits. This dependence puts them in the midst of a contradictory process of de-standardization and institutionalization (Beck, 1992). As on the one hand state institutions are based on more or less narrow assumptions regarding what constitutes the 'norm' (Böhnisch, 1994) and on the other upon bureaucratic procedures, young people in prolonged and fragmented yo-yo transitions may not fit into institutional criteria of eligibility. They may be too young or too old, unemployed for a too long or a too short time. There therefore exists what can be described as a 'socio-political vacuum' (Müller, 1996) between youth and adulthood in which increasing numbers of young women and young men are trapped. As institutional support is often neither accessible nor appropriate to complex constellations of everyday life young people have to 'invent' individual coping strategies. These necessarily do not fit into institutional logics and young people tend to be considered 'undeserving' (clearly visible in the case of rights and responsibilities with regard to the acceptance of 'any' job versus the entitlement to unemployment benefit) or even deviant, as a result.

The above leads us to a crucial point: transitions have to be analysed according to a *structural* dimension but such transitions are negotiated in an active way. The mobilization of labour markets, the decreasing employment guarantees provided by education and training, or the diversification of life conditions between autonomy and dependence on the one side remain important, but so do the shifts occurring between youth and adulthood with regard to self-concepts, decision-taking, attitudes and lifestyles, in so far as they are bound to reflect structural transitions. There are clearly ambivalences and contradictions that link structure and agency. Young people are increasingly autonomous, but at one and the same time (and despite impressions to the contrary) the scope for genuine choice is more and more constrained at a structural level.

Agency in transition

The fact that young people's transitions to adulthood are no longer straightforward or predictable means they are constantly confronted with fundamentally important existential questions: 'What does this mean to me?' 'Is this where I want to go?' Authors as Alheit (1995) and Böhnisch (1997) have referred to this as *biographization*. Under conditions of individualization biographies have to be constructed individually and this requires particular knowledge and competencies. Not surprisingly, bur perhaps misleadingly, young women and men perceive themselves as being well-informed, well-oriented, and as having no real problems (Stauber, 1999). Here we can identify important gender differences: research on female socialization and on young women's life plans has shown that girls and young women develop biographical consciousness and reflexivity very early on. Young women's life courses and trajectories in modern societies are structured by a fundamental contradiction. Culturally they are supposed, in theory at least, to have the same opportunities as men. In the relatively short period of two or three decades this has lead to the internalization of work as being a self-evident part of female life by young women. This constitutes a relatively new normality for young women. In reality, however, this new normality is constantly threatened by restricted choices, lower income and limited support structures for reconciling work and family. Young women therefore are 'experts of ambiguity'. They are constantly having to address gender inequalities, and within the 'myth of equal opportunities' (Oechsle and Geissler 1998) they constantly have to assert themselves at all levels (Leccardi, 1996; Peters and du Bois-Reymond, 1996; West and Zimmerman, 1987).

Precisely because there is an increasing tension between the reality of their living conditions and broader orientational demands, young people are obliged to find solutions. But this is easier said than done. In fact, young people are more likely to find 'imaginary solutions' (Clarke *et al.*, 1975;

Helfferich, 1994); solutions which preserve agency and subjectivity, but which can only ultimately provide a symbolic means of transcending existing transitional conditions. Short term imaginary solutions can also, however, provide young people with a means for self-actualization and are potentially motivationally important in facing up to the bigger problems. The problem with this conception of 'imaginary solutions' which stems from the 1970s British subcultural theorists is arguably that such an approach is based on hierarchical base/superstructure thinking:

> 'This traditional base/superstructure model underestimates the role of stylization, discourses and symbolic structures in society. Youth cultures have not made the revolutions some of them (the members of the Birmingham School) dreamt of, but they were more than deviations from the essentialities of life and politics. Some of their cultural experiments have contributed to important mental and ideological transformations in society, with wide but diffuse effects far beyond those people who were directly involved in them. Their contestation of 'normal' lifestyles invented new possible forms of identity, in processes that do not compete with trade unions or political parties since they are in a quite different field, but that strongly affect emancipatory potentials of future social **movements.**'
> (Fornäs, 1995, p. 108).

At the very least the sorts of 'solutions' young people pursue illustrate they are not simply passive recipients of structural change. They participate in education and training, they make decisions, whilst trying to keep their options open. And they engage in youth cultures in order to stylize and symbolize the decisions they take; as a means, in turn, of finding a place in society they consider as providing meaning. Whether these 'solutions' have positive effects as regards social integration or not – and potentially they also could be too one-dimensional and therefore prolonging young people's exclusion – they clearly show the importance of culture in a very broad sense: the importance of symbolic representation, the importance of styling, of presenting oneself and of being visible.

There is a heated and on-going debate about whether or not youth subcultures still exist. Without wishing to extend that debate our position is that the concept of *sub*-culture can still be applied in an useful way in some contexts (Hodkinson 2001). However, we would also like to stress the importance of youth lifestyles (Miles 2001) which comprise young people's cultural and stylistic interpretation of structural constraints,

> 'When identities – individual or collective, psychic, social or cultural – are mobilized and problematized, the ability and need to define oneself both

increase. Reflexivity is intense in the life phase of adolescence and youth, where childhood is to be reworked into adulthood. It is also intensified among sub- or microcultures, cultivating styles and forms of expression. And when epochal shifts are taking place, societal reflexivity is generally increased. In late modern youth culture, these focal points coincide.' (Fornäs, 1995, p. 212).

Of particular concern here is the link between general social change and the need for identity work, which is most visible in transitions between youth and adulthood. Balancing equals agency and vice versa: agency shows itself in the balancing acts young people perform on a daily basis. Studies in youth research have shown that young people's life strategies can largely be characterized by a 'step-by-step' or 'wait and see' approach. Young people appear to want to negotiate and compromise with formal institutions, whilst keeping their options open at the same time (Evans and Heinz, 1994; Pais, 1995; Buzzi *et al.*, 1997; Walther, 2000). At the same time, they are making everyday decisions that potentially have long term implications for their futures (Müller, 1996; Walther, 2000). In this context, self-presentation and symbolic production provide an important means of asserting a person's self-identity.

There is indeed an argument for suggesting that post-modern identities are about actively negotiating flexibility and commitment. Youth lifestyles often reflect the fragmented nature of both youth identities and the transitional systems in which such identities are constructed. Patchwork styles, for example, symbolize the need to stay flexible, to call on *different* reference points, to avoid being fixed to one style, to one decision and to one biographic model. They illustrate the need to maintain the capacity to changed situations, to stay flexible, to live what are in effect, patchwork biographies (Alheit, 1996).

Patchwork biographies and forms of self-representation seem to be closely connected: the first being much less a matter of choice than structurally forced, the latter representing the means by which young people can cope with the first. Because class divisions are arguably less clear-cut than they used to be, lifestyles might well be described as 'individualized symbols of social reproduction' (Bourdieu, 1989; Neckel, 1991). The agency involved here can therefore range from high risk patterns of agency to rather adaptive 'mainstream' ones. It would therefore be too simplistic to idealize youth lifestyles, which are necessarily contradictory in nature.

Nevertheless, *performativity* reveals to become a central issue in late modern transitions (Bauman 1995), and youth lifestyles allow young people to work with their patchwork biographies, because they offer opportunity structures for self-representation and self-performance. In this context, we can identify a broad range of needs on the part of young people:

- the need for a sense of belonging, which itself reflects the arguably over-individualized nature of the transition process;
- the need for a sense of meaning and relevance which could emerge from communal agency (Beck/Beck-Gernsheim 1994);
- the need for a sense of coherence (Antonovsky, 1987), which has been identified as the general core topic of all 'identity work' (cf. Keupp, 1997), and which, in turn, reflects the apparent fragmentation of different spheres of life.

It is this framework of needs and their concerning structural backgrounds where youth lifestyles, young people's imaginary solutions, performing and self-representing activities have to be located. Otherwise discourses about these topics run the risk of simply reproducing a discourse of individualization.

In the research upon which this book is based we were concerned with the impact of cultural expression upon young people's transitions. This also has to be seen in the wider context of structurally changed transitions:

'The main reason for the increased centrality of culture among young people as well as adults is probably the problematization and intensification of identity work. The needs to formulate one's personal and social identity grow, as identity constructions are denaturalized, and it is through cultural discourses that relations and positions are negotiated.' (Fornäs, 1995, p. 215).

We do not want to equate identity work with all cultural phenomena, but we want to say that *potentially*, and especially in youth transitions, cultural expressions are closely related to identity work, providing an important source of belonging, meaning and coherence. They represent spaces of experimentation and allow young people to construct their own biographies.

Social innovation and transformation have to be located at least partly at the level of everyday agency. This is especially true in the case of young people whose agency continues to be underestimated. The intention of the research discussed here is to begin to come to terms with some of the needs young people have in an ever changing world: the need to belong and to feel secure and in control of their own lives. It is for these reasons young people's cultural orientations and practices have to be taken into account when researching youth transitions. They are not simply relevant in terms of the construction of individual identity, but also as social arenas that interface with transition systems. Unfortunately these areas remain undersupported insofar as they lack institutional recognition. The training mindset is such that the acquisition of competencies or potential employment are key concerns. The less explicit benefits to be had from the training process are therefore neglected. Training agencies, understandably prioritize measurable outputs, but by doing so undermine the effectiveness and potential richness of the training they provide.

Biographical learning under conditions of uncertainty

In the above sections we have tried to highlight the fact that in recent years young people's transitions have become increasingly de-standardized. Young people's transitions are almost inevitably uncertain. In this context, the relationship between social integration and transitions in general needs to be re-defined. Standardized institutional ways of channelling young peoples' transitions provide a systematic means of integration as Giddens (1984) notes. Such mechanisms represent societies' efforts to generalize rules and resources of social integration (Giddens, 1984). In turn, as Habermas (1981) argues, in periods of social change rationalized forms of direct social integration are embedded in individuals' life worlds and everyday lives. The general objective of the research project documented here can be understood as a search for social situations in which such rationalization processes are located. In other words, the key question here is concerned with the extent to which learning processes and learning situations actually provide young people with the skills and competencies they need in a changing world. There is a distinct possibility that more formal structured programmes are failing young people. What are the alternatives?

Social space and performance

When referring to the concept of *'empowerment'* (Rappaport et. al., 1984) in the remainder of this document we are concerned with the extent to which young women and young men are provided with resources, spaces, and opportunities to improve their coping strategies and to acquire the competencies they perceive to be necessary in this regard. We would even like to concretise the notion of empowerment by talking about the key prerequisites for agency: social space and social competencies. According to du Bois-Reymond and Walther (1999) it is mainly young people with higher qualifications who receive acknowledgement for informally acquired competencies. In turn, such young people apparently go on to realize the wider social value of such competencies managing to integrate them in a strategic manner with their more formal qualifications. More generally the benefits of informal learning effects tend to be underestimated. As far as this project is concerned it seems entirely plausible that performing arts constitute an important space in which young people can experiment with expressive styles and forms of self-representation. Theatre work with its emphasis on performance can be said to represent an appropriate means of bringing young people 'out of themselves'. Performance provides a context within which young people can balance complimentary aspects of formal learning, cultural style and expression, and individual circumstances. Performance allows young people to link their cultural practices to their life plans, as young men and women, and lifestyles in a biographically coherent fashion. It is therefore very important that young people develop a sense of 'biographicity'.

> 'Biographicity means that we can redesign again and again, from scratch, the contours of our life within the specific contexts in which we (have to) spend it, and that we experience these contexts as 'shapeable' and designable.' (Alheit, 1995, p. 65).

Based on the distinction of different ways of learning suggested by Finger (1988) Stroobants connects (1999) the concept of 'biographicity' to different perspectives individuals take towards society:

> 'When society is viewed as something new and unknown which one wants to make oneself familiar with, one learns to acquire new ways to adapt to society. When society is perceived as strange and threatening, one wants to define oneself in contrast with it, emancipating from it. When society is considered as different, a dynamic confrontation can come about wherein the individual can take up an active social role. This way of looking at the learning processes of people makes way for innovative learning based on how adults are able to – and how they acquire new knowledge and competencies to – guide their lives, make innovations and participate in society.'(Manninen, 1998)' (Stroobants, 1999, p. 134).

Our hypothesis is that performing arts carry a high potential for young people in developing a sense of biographicity. Individual perceptions and interpretations have to be expressed in the public sphere, either in the context of a group or in front of an audience. This exchange between the internal 'self' and external feedback potentially leads to the very core of biographicity: it provides a context in which individual life histories can be legitimized. In this setting and in this social network young people are able to relate individual experiences and orientations to the local opportunity structure as regards, education, training and employment. In short young people can play out their own biographies in a creative context in which those biographies are accepted and nourished.

Self-confidence is a central aspect of personal motivation: the belief that by own action subjectively relevant goals may be achieved (Heckhausen, 1990). Once again performing arts appear to constitute an excellent medium for encouraging such confidence. This, of course presupposes that young people are utterly committed to achieving such goals. In order to achieve such an aim, and in the context of projects we looked at in this study, we can see the advantages of participatory curricula, where topics of young peoples' concern are prioritized, and where they can reflect upon themselves a both performers and human beings; an experience which forms an important contrast to their daily life. Self-confidence is not something that either does or does not exist. It is the product of the learning process. This learning processes is potentially aggravated or even prevented by traditional (and arguably far too common) educational and training settings. It is therefore important to create more stimulating learning situations, where this kind of indirect learning is facilitated. It is very important that young people are provided with settings which encourage them to have faith in themselves. This is not usually the case in systems that invest so much in more formal modes of training. In short, as this report will go on to illustrate, the process of the training and the extent to which that process becomes personal to the individual 'consumer' of that training is potentially far more important than any discrete measures of skill acquisition that far too often prioritize the needs of the trainer, while almost entirely forgetting the needs of the 'trained'.

In concluding this section it is worth reiterating the fact that this project is concerned with coming to terms with the sorts of conditions that promote a more pragmatic and beneficial form of learning that has young people's needs (which will very often directly fulfil economic ones) at its core.

> 'How far different cultural settings allow a 'faith' in the coherence of everyday life through providing symbolic interpretations of existential questions is... very important. But cognitive frames of meaning will not generate that faith without a corresponding level of underlying emotional commitment – whose origins... are largely unconscious. Trust, hope and courage are all relevant to such commitment.' (Giddens, 1991, p. 37).

Ontological security lies at the centre of the above argument. In a world of uncertainty young people will have considerable difficulty in 'finding

themselves'. Youth training should play a key role in this process. Performing arts potentially provides an arena diverse and stimulating enough to
promote this sense of ontological security. In this setting, meaningful rou-
tines are first: developed, secondly, rehearsed and finally, expressed in
public. Through this process individual's identities are legitimised. This is
largely a question of confidence. In order to increase their self-confidence
young people must:

- have the opportunity to experiment with expressive means in an environment which is both safe and supportive;
- have the opportunity to take responsibility for their own choices and
  actions in order that they can foster their own sense of 'control';
- be commended for their strengths and competencies which cannot, as
  such be taken for granted. Young people's achievements should not be
  assumed. Rather they should be celebrated.

In Chapter 4, empirical evidence will be presented as a means of assessing
the potential of performing arts in the context of the above conceptual
mdiscussion. Special attention will be paid to how far the arts themselves
are empowering and to the role played by the *informal* nature of learning
contexts and processes. What role do less formal training programmes actually play? Is it actually an exaggeration to claim that such training
actively encourages young people as subjective authors (and thus benefici-
aries) of their own training?

Chapter 3

Researching Communities of Youth: Some thoughts on methodology

In the previous chapter, we laid out the theoretical concepts which underlie this research. We argued that youth transitions had to be seen in the wider context of the apparently de-standardized and protracted nature of 'youth'. If we accept that the nature of youth is indeed, in some sense, changing then it is worth considering the implications of these changes for how best to investigate young people's experiences, before specifically addressing the question of how we went about researching 'communities of youth'. Our perspective on 'youth' is underpinned by the suggestion that youth is not simply a status passage, some form of a means to an end, but constitutes a significant period in people's lives in it's own right. From this point of view research can not and should not focus on how far young people succeed in 'accomplishing' the transition from youth to adulthood. It should rather seek to understand the criteria young people develop to assess and navigate through their current situations. In this context, the ways in which young people invest their own meanings in the learning experience can be related to wider questions of social integration. This will help to counter-balance the limitations of the 'problem-oriented' approach normally associated with 'disadvantaged' youth which has an overwhelming tendency to ignore the actual 'voices' and competencies of young people.

By giving young people the opportunity to express themselves they are in a position to demonstrate their strengths and competencies, but are also more confident about discussing any weaknesses they may feel they have. In this way young people's own sense of reality can be factored into the research process. On the other hand, taking such a stance could help in bridging the gap between culturally informed approaches which sometimes over-emphasize the expressive agentic aspects of young people's lives and more structurally-oriented approaches which often neglect aspects of active meaning making by young men and women. In our considered opinion many of the 'blind spots' of current youth research are the direct result of an inability or reluctance to address this methodological issue. With a stronger orientation towards the actual life worlds of young people research can gain a more complete and more 'realistic' image of young people's lives. Youth research therefore needs to develop subtle and innovative research strategies that can transcend conventional limitations to bring these complex issues to light. It is also worth remembering that young people tend to have a high degree of sensitivity when it comes to the mechanics of the interview situation. They may actively seek to conceal anything that they perceive may portray them in a negative light. Research that takes the problematic as its starting point is more liable to construct a misleading picture of what it means to be a young person. An approach that self-consciously avoids the problematic has at least a reasonable chance of surmounting these difficulties.

The methodology chosen in the context of this research tries to access the nature of the learning experience through the analysis of the training process and the actual biographical nature of that process. It did not aim to 'prove' a relationship between learning effects, participation and attitudes, but attempted to look beneath the surface of those learning processes which occurred during participation. We therefore set out to give young people the space in which they could express their own experience of the particular training in which they were engaged. This approach can be described as a form of action research: the young women and men themselves determined the dynamics of the projects in which they participated and, in this sense, also determined the dynamics of this research. The main intention of the research instruments we used was to give young people the space to express concerns that would not normally be accessible through a more conventional approach.

The basic hypothesis upon which we based this fieldwork was that, potentially at least, the performing arts provide a means of empowering young people by facilitating a different kind of learning to that which is normally associated with more conventional training strategies. Such strategies are far more likely to discourage and de-motivate. Conventional training schemes find it very difficult to engage with young people. In effect, there is a significant gap in communication between the institutions and their target audience. In effect, what we were aiming at was what Michael Patton (1989) once called an 'illuminative evaluation' rather than a summative evaluation, with the key objective being to evaluate the projects' effectiveness in training young people. The research rationale behind such an approach is concerned more with tracing young people's actual experience and relating it to their structural circumstances than with evaluating the outcomes of the projects in terms of whether or not the young people concerned acquire a set of skills to be ticked off against a rigid check-list. The aim of the field work was to gain insight into the above through the following key questions:

- What can we understand about the learning processes which take place in socio-cultural projects?
- What conditions and prerequisites are required for the success of such projects?
- What benefits might a trans-national approach provide in terms of enlightening our understanding of youth training and, more specifically, aspects of informal learning?

With these questions in mind we wanted to generate a kind of 'local situated knowledge', as Lave and Wenger (1991) put it, which might help us come to terms with the relationship between the meanings young people invested in the learning process and the institutional and curricular setting that underpinned that learning process. As a means of understanding these complex relationships we set about understanding how young people prepared for and partook in a performance, and related this to the biographical and institutional surroundings of the earning process.

A case study approach

As a means of addressing the above issues we selected a different youth project in each of our three countries. The reasons for choosing these particular projects were in part pragmatic: we were familiar with all three projects from earlier research and evaluation projects, and we knew that each project represented a manifestation of the research questions we were seeking to develop. The second reason for our choice was the mixture of similarity and variation and hence the compatibility of the three projects. Lying at the heart of this research is the common philosophy associated with informal training: the underlying ideology, pedagogical and practical approach and, last but not least, how, in effect, this form of training is 'consumed' by young people themselves. But the differences between the three projects are as significant as their similarities (see Chapter 5); the most important difference between the projects perhaps being the strategic position they occupy in their respective transition systems. By pursuing these case studies we were able to come to terms with the broader national variations associated with what are, after all, very different systems.

The case studies we have conducted rely entirely on a qualitative methodology. This reflects our contention that a more quantitative approach to

inter-cultural comparison, though tempting, was likely to be far more su-
perficial than an in-depth qualitative approach which, in turn, is likely to
glean a richer set of results. Bearing the above in mind we developed what
could be described as three 'instrumental' case studies (Stake, 1994); in
other words the case study approach allowed us to address more abstract
issues in a practical context. This is in direct contrast to what have been
referred to as 'intrinsic' case studies where the case studies simply stand for
themselves.

The specific questions we wanted our case studies to answer were as
follows:

- how far do the three projects work for the young people concerned?
- how effective is their work with regard to providing prerequisites for
  young people to withstand the sort of problems we associate with transitions to adulthood?
- which elements of the three projects might usefully be transferred and
  applied to mainstream training and youth policies?

These questions were operationalized on three levels of field work: the institutional level, the organizational level and the biographical level. These
different levels covered different aspects of the core research question, but
they were also used as means to triangulate the findings.

**The institution: expert interviews, participant observation and
documentary analysis**

On this level we were interested in finding out how the projects operated as
organizations. In the first instance, we were thus concerned with the concepts and methodologies the projects used in their work with young people.
Second, we were interested in their relationship with the institutional setting in which they operated. Third, we wanted to find out which
assumptions and visions were underpinning these organizations: could we
find traces of 'institutional reflexivity'? Did the institutions concerned actively reflect upon the changing demands arising from the changing nature
of young people's biographies (Walther *et al.*, 2002)? To this end, 'key
persons' were interviewed: pedagogical staff members, project managers,
i.e. persons whose role it was to facilitate young people's experience of the
training process. Semi-structured interviews (with a common interview
schedule) were conducted with a key person in each location. In terms of
interview technique and attitude each researcher, broadly speaking, adopted

the approach developed by Kvale (1996). The interviews were therefore focused, but nonetheless loosely structured in nature. In addition, we studied the historical development and pedagogical principles of each of the three projects through documentary analysis (cf. Hodder, 1994). We also used observation as a means of evaluating the training process. This required frequent visits to project workshops and public performances. Finally we also felt it was very important to feedback our results to each of the projects in order that this research had practical implications at more than one level.

The training group: focus groups and participant observation

On the conceptual level, we were interested in how the pedagogical model adopted by each of the projects actually 'worked': what, to begin with, made each of the project's attractive to each of its participants? What meanings did they ascribe to their participation? How did they interpret their experiences of their particular course? Our aim was to examine the quality of the learning processes in each project. In order to achieve this aim we needed an approach that ensured the participation of a high degree of those people involved in each of the projects. The reflections of the young people themselves were deemed as important, in fact if anything, more important, than those responsible for providing the training.

Focus groups consisting of project participants were used to investigate the learning experiences and subjective meanings which young people drew from their participation in these courses. Focus groups are an especially good means of assessing collective and interactive processes of meaning construction (Miles, 1996; Morgan, 1997). They actively encourage participants to develop and articulate opinions in a social situation that is similar to the one under discussion. The group serves as a 'safe space': the hierarchy between interviewers and interviewees is minimized, and the interviewer acts as a facilitator rather than a 'conductor' of the interview. This allows for more of a natural discussion to develop than is possible in the more artificial contexts in which one-to-one interviews tend to be conducted. Group interviews encourage the development of a relaxed relationship with interviewees. The group situation also tends to enliven and stimulate participants and to integrate them as active research participants.

The individual: biographical interviews

If our starting point is that biography and identity are intimately related to the comparative success of the learning process, it follows that that learning process can only be effectively assessed by giving the participants the opportunity to re-construct their learning experiences within the context of their own biography. To find out how the experience of the participants was related to their biographies and individual trajectories we therefore conducted biographical interviews with individual participants (Kvale, 1996). The interview method used was derived from the 'issue-centred' interview which was, in turn, originally developed by Witzel *et al.* (1982). Basically, this method consists of a semi-structured interview focused around a central theme. This method has proven to be especially appropriate in a transnational setting insofar as it allowed us to ask specific contextual questions whilst pursuing a common theme. We developed our themes and questions as part of an on-going discussion in order to ensure comparability. The biographical interviews were tape-recordęd, transcribed and evaluated according to a common scheme of interpretation.

Symbolic production: analysing the performances

Each of the methods described here represent just one constituent element of the overall evaluation. As such, it is important to reflect on how, if it all, the chosen methodologies, complimented one another. An analysis of a performance was deemed significant insofar as it allowed us to consider the 'outputs' of each of the three projects. In analysing our data we endeavoured to reconstruct the learning processes of the participants and the circumstances that had contributed to these processes. This approach reflects that of Denzin (1989) who developed his own qualitative methodology for the analysis of video and film materials. Given that the products (the scenes put on stage by the drama group) were fixed on videotape this approach proved ideally suitable for an analysis of drama productions. Because this aspect of the research constitutes the least familiar of the methods we have deployed in this project we will consider its step-by-step use in more detail:

- Each of the three projects in Liverpool, Lisbon and Mannheim initiated, developed and rehearsed a new performance during the period of time this research covers. We used this period for frequent visits to attend rehearsals, conduct interviews with the participants and experts who were either from within, or associated with the projects. Once the performances were complete, we made a video tape of the scenes developed by each project and used it as a key to analyse the training process in action.

- An important prerequisite for any qualitative analysis is to be aware of one's analytical categories. Therefore broad theory-based research questions and theoretical concepts were formulated before the analysis started.

- The first step of analysis consisted of a macro-analysis of the whole video-tape during which we looked for key sequences and themes. On the surface, the end product constituted in a particular scene is not of particular use in itself, but the analysis of that end product can provide a way into understanding the nature of the learning process. In all three instances, the young people concerned played a key role in the decision-making process that lay behind the construction of specific scenes. It can therefore be argued that the learning process reflects the investment young people make in that process. By understanding the meaning and intention of single scenes we were able to go at least some way towards addressing the meanings underpinning the performance. The tapes were watched as a whole and detailed notes outlining first impressions and direct interpretations of the contents were taken. In a second run through of the tape those sequences illustrating thematic issues were identified.

- The identified thematic fields were then developed into questions broadly concerned with the development of the performance. In the German example for instance, one of the questions resulting from the analysis was concerned with why the young people chose a traditional family conflict in Sicily as a topic for their drama work. Another question dealt with how it came to be that the young men took over female roles in the play? With guiding questions like these single sequences and their development were submitted to what Denzin (1989, p. 231) calls 'structured micro-analysis' in order to identify patterns of expression that lead to certain sequences in the play.

- The choice of key sequences served as a structure for a group interview with the participants. The interview questions were linked thematically to the key sequences of the play, thereby creating a common concern between the researcher and the participant, something that is often lacking in 'artificially' created interview situations. The common interpretation of the play and of the meaning and artistic intention of the key sequences was used to reconstruct the learning experiences of the participants. Like the drama itself this method offered a means of accessing these young people's real living conditions and their personal experiences.

- The answers to the guiding questions were formulated and discussed together with the staff member who was therefore able to bring his or her pedagogical insight into play. On a second level of interpretation the key sequences of the play were shown to the trans-national research team and analysed along commonly developed patterns of interpretation.

This detailed account illustrates the ways we tried to link the different levels of investigation in a hermeneutic process which comprised several steps where data from other sources such as the biographical interviews could be contrasted with the end product of the performance. In this way we took advantage of the opportunity to re-consider our findings and our analysis, whilst challenging any assumptions we might have made along the way.

Intercultural interpretation and comparison

During our attempt to bridge the gap between the discourses of changing youth identities and lifestyles on the one hand and youth transitions and learning on the other, the nature of trans-national comparison (alongside questions of multi-disciplinarity) became a guiding principle of the research. There is a long-standing methodological discussion going on in sociological research on the merits and problems of comparative studies. It is generally agreed that cross-national and cross-cultural research is valuable for establishing the generality of a theory and the validity of findings. But at the same time almost insurmountable theoretical and methodological problems can arise in the process of establishing a focus for the research, controlling variables and balancing cultural variations in the definition of concepts (Inkeles and Sasaki, 1996; Oyen, 1990).

A particular concern of ours was how to and what to compare: individuals, or groups of individuals living in different regions with different properties, or nations (Scheuch, 1990)? In our project we attempted to incorporate all three levels of analysis. Kohn (1996) in an influential article on cross-national research as an analytical strategy, distinguishes between nations as the object of study, as opposed to nations as the *context* of study. In the latter case, 'one is primarily interested in testing the generality of findings and interpretations about how certain social institutions operate or about certain aspects of social structure impinge on personality' (Kohn, 1996: p. 29). Our project self-consciously takes the three countries national transitions systems as its starting point. From this basis we intend to take into account the macro as well as the micro. A first step in trying to reduce the complexity of such an approach is to address national patterns as they are expressed in the local context through case studies such as those presented here. Thus, our evaluation is concerned with the nature of the links between a certain type of learning and the ways in which that learning is enabled. Therefore, the point of reference between the three projects is the fact that they are atypical as compared to mainstream forms of training normally associated with the education and training system in which they operate.

Our chosen case studies were not intended to be in any way representative of either their host countries or the particular transition systems operating in those countries. In contrast, we contend that the quality of our research is premised on the qualities and unique characteristics of the three projects under discussion. We therefore invested a considerable amount of time in understanding and contextualizing the three projects, in order that we could establish a rigorous conceptual and analytical framework. We feel that cross-cultural comparison has, in this case, provided an invaluable means of avoiding the parochial limitations of more geographically limited research projects. The variation in transition systems and the differences between the three projects therefore actively enriched the research process (see EGRIS, 2001; Bennett, 1999).

A key second step was concerned with *how* to compare: as Hübner-Funk and du Bois-Reymond (1995) point out, comparative research of this kind often involves the rather awkward juxtaposition of descriptions of national data linking them with loosely related structural indicators, without the benefit of common theoretical concepts which would enable a more sophisticated form of comparison. Hübner-Funk and du Bois-Reymond contrast this 'additive' type of European youth research to a more promising 'integrated' approach in which the European perspective is liberating rather than restrictive (see Hübner-Funk and du Bois-Reymond, 1995: pp. 262-264). We tried to ensure this was the case during this research by incorporating detailed discussions about the concepts we would operationalize, about different approaches and about the implications of commonly used notions. These discussions were seen to be a very important part of the process to ensure that each of the three research partners were working in tandem.

Although our aim is to compare the relative benefits of the three projects, it is important to recognize that each of them operate within different conditions and circumstances. These differences had to be borne in mind in order to maximize the benefits to be had from a comparative analysis of this kind. It was also particularly crucial that the research was carefully synchronized with common research methods and regular exchanges regarding the way in which the research was developing in each of the partner countries. Without neglecting any differences that might crop up in our own specific projects, we carefully followed a common methodological agenda. We also made sure, as far as possible, that there were no 'gaps' or inconsistencies in our existing procedures. In effect, we used each other as an extra 'pair of eyes and ears' by not confining the comparison to nationally specific interpretations, but by utilizing a common interpretation of the data. Nonetheless, our data is presented according to the specific findings of the three projects. Each project is evaluated according to the common structure established by the researchers as a group (see Chapter 4). Because all these projects are exceptions in their respective national and local contexts, they cannot be compared in any direct fashion. Therefore the findings of the case studies are presented one-by-one. Each case study presentation starts with a description and explanation of the transition systems in which the respective project operates. The specific nature of each project within these broader conditions are then discussed. This analysis provides a backdrop against which we turn back to the more theoretical inter-cultural comparison which we began to develop in Chapter 2.

Chapter 4

Case Studies

The German case study

The labour market situation

The unemployment rate for young people in Germany has for a long time has been the lowest in Europe and, indeed, lower than the national unemployment rate. Since the early 1990s however young people have experienced an increased risk of unemployment in their transition from school to work due to a major decline of training and employment opportunities. In 1998 the unemployment rate for under 25 year olds rose to 11.8 per cent compared to a national average of 12.3 per cent (Bundesanstalt, 1999). In contrast to other European countries, unemployment rates in Germany do not appear to fall after the age of 25. As such, youth unemployment carries a high risk of continuous exclusion and subsequently the degree of that exclusion might, in decades to come, penetrate older age groups.

Three key structural elements of youth unemployment in Germany have to be considered: first, the labour market has been affected by the unification of Germany in 1989. Economic restructuring has created a sharp imbalance between East and West (youth unemployment at 17 per cent in the East compared to 10 per cent in the West). Second, the core of the vocational training system, the dual system (see below), which has been responsible for the low rate of youth unemployment by channelling youth transitions through protected pathways, has suffered a heavy decline as regards the supply of apprenticeship places. This problem has been exacerbated by a parallel contraction of the labour market in Germany. Third, the segmentation of labour markets and the training system leads to an unequal distribution of unemployment risks. Only minor gender differences can be identified: in 1997 there was a higher unemployment rate for females under 20 year olds (9.6 per cent of males and 11.0 per cent of females in the West, 14.8 per cent versus 20.1 per cent in the East). Amongst 20 to 25 year olds, western males were affected to a higher extent than females (13.9 per cent versus 9.9 per cent), whereas in the East no significant gender differences occurred (21.7 per cent and 22.0 per cent). However, it should also be noted that there is also a higher rate of inactive females, while young people from ethnic minorities are twice as likely to be unenmployed as their counterparts (Bundesanstalt 1999).

The structure of the German transition system

The German transition system is based on a highly selective school system: after four years pupils are selected according to individual achievement in elementary education. They then follow one of three routes, each of which differs considerably as regards social status and later training and employ-ment prospects. It is also important to note that education and training is organized regionally in Germany and that the rigidity of this selection proc-ess will therefore vary. The basic Secondary School (Hauptschule) leads to the Certificate of Compulsory Education after five years, the Middle Sec-ondary School (Realschule) provides a certificate of a higher status after six years and this particular qualification is considered to be the 'educational minimum' for an apprenticeship in most professions (Zenke, 1995). Only the Grammar School (Gymnasium) provides a qualification (Abitur) that will allow young people to access higher education. In 1997 8.8 per cent of pupils left school without any qualification, 26.8 per cent with the basic qualification, 39.7 per cent with the next level of certification and 24.7 per cent with the 'Abitur' leading to higher education. There is a clear gender division underlying these statistics. The majority of those achieving middle and higher qualifications are female, while males dominate at the least qualified end of the scale. Ethnicty also has a significant impact on the sta-tistics: the percentage of young people from ethnic minorities with no and basic qualifications is twice as high as the national average (Statistisches Bundesamt, 1999).

School to work transitions in Germany are characterized by two thresh-olds: the 'first threshold' from school to vocational training, and the 'second threshold' from vocational training to employment. The system of vocational training has a major role in regulating youth transitions. Ap-proximately 65 per cent of all school leavers enter the dual system of apprenticeship, i.e. a three and half year company-based practical training combined with general and vocational education in professional schools. Apprenticeship contracts are made between young people and companies, thus giving them access to the social insurance system and assuring an ap-prenticeship wage. However, since the late 1980s companies started to withdraw from the dual system, thus leading to a heavy decline in the sup-ply of apprenticeship places. In doing so, companies tried to reduce labour costs and to be more flexible. In addition, this decline illustrates the fact that the dual system was dependent on the manufacturing and crafts sector. Unfortunately, no adequate training opportunities have been developed in the service sector (Baethge, 1999). Meanwhile, due to the slow process of restructuring in East Germany a training infrastructure could only be developed with huge state support. 90 per cent of all apprenticeship places therefore depended on public funding, while 25 per cent of all apprenticeship were provided in surrogate training workshops. East German young people are at a high risk of failing at the 'second threshold'; in other words, those young people who have secured an apprenticeship are still likely to be unemployed (BMBF 1999).

In the above context, the crisis of the dual system can therefore be said to promote three major patterns:

- *Education*: Increased competition and a shift towards more theoretical content has meant that there has been a general qualification inflation which has seen grammar school leavers leaving those with basic qualifications in their wake.
- *Gender*: the lower percentage of young women in the dual system (approximately 40 per cent) has been maintained through the decline of training opportunities; young women have therefore tended to orient themselves towards school-based training courses, typically in those areas or professions most commonly associated with women such as health and social welfare.
- *Ethnicity*: young people with a migration background have considerable difficulty passing the 'first threshold'. Only 40 per cent enter vocational training (see BMBF 1999).

An additional concern related to the crisis of the dual system is the high rate of drop-outs: more than 20 per cent of the apprenticeship contracts are rejected prior to certification, most of them within the first six months. A high percentage of young people therefore run the risk of not finding another apprenticeship place and/or are too discouraged to aspire to gain those qualifications deemed necessary to enter the labour market (BMBF, 1999). High drop-out rates at this stage can be explained by increased aspirations (due to higher qualifications and individualized life plans) and the pressures that young people are under, notably from parents, to enter 'any' apprenticeship in order to avoid unemployment and social exclusion. Many professional choices are taken for 'fear of falling' rather then because they represent the appropriate choice for that individual at a given time (Ehrenreich, 1991). Only after some months do many young people realize that their chosen profession does not suit them at all. In this situation, the long duration of apprenticeship appears to young people to simply waste their time. The lack of a genuine modular system within which young people would have a large degree of personal choice results in a situation in which young people have to take serious decisions that are not easily reversible without the risk of social exclusion.

The considerable pressure under which young people have to make occupational choices and biographical decisions has ensured that *vocational counselling* has come to play a key role in maintaining the link between school and training. Vocational training is part of the national employment service and its tasks are to: provide information and orientation, counselling, and to place applicants in apprenticeships. Vocational orientation starts in the last two years before leaving school and mainly consists of visiting the information and documentation centres and in short-term 3 – 10 day placements in companies. Vocational counsellors are under considerable pressure to channel applicants to the available apprenticeship places. Thus, the space for individual aspirations and ambitions is very much limited by institutional prerogatives. Young people, as well as youth workers and social workers therefore often criticize the vocational counselling for failing to respect individual needs and for the limited time available for individual counselling (see Behrens and Brown, 1994; Nuglisch and Pfendtner, 1998).

If we accept that training opportunities are limited it is necessary to consider the alternative options currently available to young people. For school leavers under 18 years of age one compulsory year of vocational education in a professional school is compulsory. Those leaving school with a basic or middle qualification, but not entering vocational training have to attend a year of pre-vocational education (again there are regional differences with regard to available alternatives). The *school-based pre-vocational year* (BVJ) does not lead to any additional qualifications. Students are considered to be not 'mature for training'. Students in these classes come from a diversity of migrant backgrounds and tend to have limited language skills, and very low qualification levels. Nevertheless most teachers are not prepared to deal with individual problems or to tailor their teaching towards individual needs.

Beside the school-based pre-vocational year there are a variety of measures and schemes for young people who have not yet entered regular training or are unemployed. Most of these measures are co-ordinated by voluntary organizations which are organized in Germany by big welfare corporations affiliated to the churches, the trade unions or the Red Cross. This 'parallel system' of *'vocational youth assistance'* ('Jugendsozialarbeit') is funded either regionally by the employment service, or by local authorities. The major objective of vocational youth assistance is to bring young people identified as 'disadvantaged' back into the regular system of training and employment by addressing their individual deficiencies, as opposed to diversifying accepted and acknowledged pathways to regular work. Correspondingly, the (learning and working) contents of the schemes are often rather low and related to manual work, rather than 'professional' in nature. Rather than actually boosting their career prospects, many young people therefore find themselves stigmatized by such schemes. Ironically, in these circumstances young people feel pressured to pursue a policy of disengagement and de-motivation. However, on the other hand, as no alternative paths towards regular employment are available, many young people accept these measures as their last chance. A significant problem with this system is that projects and project workers tend to reproduce the tendency towards disengagement: they often underestimate the qualifications and experiences of participants and ascribe motivational problems as individual shortcomings. The limited appeal of the experience provided for young people in this situation is simply justified by pointing to the need of the disadvantaged 'to learn what it really means to work'. Although very few evaluations on mid- and long-term destinations of participants have been undertaken, estimated success rates (i.e. placement in training or employment after participation) are between 20 per cent and 40 per cent (e.g. Galuske 1993; Haunert and Lang 1994; Schäfer 1997). Nevertheless, the increasing role of vocational youth assistance in the context of declining training opportunities is documented in the government's national action plan: in 1998 approximately 400,000 young people under 25 have been participating in schemes and measures funded by the employment service. It can be estimated that measures funded by other programmes accounted for about the same amount (National Action Plan, 1999).

The problem here seems to be that approaches and educational philosophies which might be perceived to be more appropriate to young people's own needs, such as youth work for example, are not recognized as pedagogically relevant. Projects addressing young people's personal biographical needs through individual counselling do not attract additional funding. Neither are the informal benefits gleaned through youth work acknowledged or accredited as part of an individual's qualifications profile.

In 1998, the in-coming government implemented an 'emergency programme' under the title '100,000 jobs for the young' to reduce youth unemployment. With 1 billion EURO per year it is a significant political gesture acknowledging the problem constituted by youth transitions. Ironically, however, the policies incorporated in this programme actually appear to reproduce the structure of the current transition system: increasing the number of apprenticeship places and pre-vocational measures. The only genuine innovation is the introduction of job creation schemes, i.e. wage subsidies for employers. Previously these schemes were restricted to individuals receiving unemployment benefit. Because of being conditioned by prior payments to the social insurance, i.e. regular work, many young unemployed people were automatically ineligible. An additional innovation is the introduction of outreach measures for disengaged young people in order to influence their orientation towards training and work. However, the limitations of vocational counselling in this context suggests the need for more experimental approaches.

The above changes in the system and in particular the one yearly basis of the new programme do nothing to address the normative assumptions and objectives which appear to underpin the German system. First, The German transition system can be characterized as strongly *normalizing* in nature. It is structured by powerful assumptions about the normality of work and of gendered life-courses. With regard to work this means the hegemony of work as 'vocational' ('Beruf'). The system places a strong emphasis on an extended commitment to training and to the acquisition of an occupational identity. Full-time and life-long careers are therefore the norm. The assumption that such work is 'normal' is a highly male-oriented one, and exacerbates a situation in which new training opportunities towards employment in the service economy are precluded (Paul-Kohlhoff 1998; Baethge 1999). Anything other than full time employment is simply not socially acceptable.

The above, in turn leads to a situation in which young people's transition problems have to be dealt with on an individual basis. Therefore, the concept of 'disadvantage' is a powerful notion in the German transition system, serving as it does as a crucial rationale for funding procedures. In the German context it is important to consider that 'disadvantage' refers to the individual circumstances behind unemployment and not to the consequences of unemployment such as poverty. Therefore support mainly consists of compensatory education and training which is based on the assumption that the higher the qualification the lower the risk of unemployment. This system therefore appears to address the symptoms rather than the cause of unemployment. The system of employment itself is not perceived to be in need of change. Rather the problem is seen to lie in the individual deficiencies of those who are unemployed. In addition policies are increasingly predetermined by a discourse of individual 'rights and responsibilities'. Recipients of unemployment and social benefit are therefore under pressure to accept 'any' job, apprenticeship or scheme. If not their benefits are liable to be drastically cut.

The JUST project

Mannheim is an industrial city of approximately 300,000 inhabitants and is located in the region of Baden-Württemberg. Badly affected by problems of de-industrialization it has the highest unemployment rate in the region and is characterized more generally by a dynamic economic structure and relatively low unemployment. In 1998 the unemployment rate in Mannheim was 13.5 per cent (compared to 8 per cent in the region of Baden-Württemberg and 12.3 per cent nationally; Bundesanstalt, 1999). This situation is also reflected by the fact that 4,500 apprenticeship applicants competed for 3,500 available places (Lattacz-Blume, 2000). It is mostly young people from ethnic minorities who are over-represented amongst the unemployed and those who fail in their ambition to enter vocational training.

Project description JUST is a community youth work project located in an inner city neighbourhood of Mannheim in Southern Germany. It was set up in 1994, at a time when youth unemployment and the consumption of hard drugs was rising, notably amongst the young immigration population. It is run by a community centre which offers a variety of social services to a variety of neighbourhood groups. The neighbourhood itself has a particular social and urban structure which is typical for neighbourhoods on the periphery of inner cities in Western Germany:

- a high density of population, and a poor infrastructure (old houses, low standard flats);
- a high density of road traffic and a lack of parks and leisure facilities;
- a high proportion of economically underprivileged households.

Equally significant is the high proportion of people from an ethnic background who live in the neighbourhood. Of particular interest is the fact that 83 per cent of young people up to the age of 21 are not of German descent.

Since the 1970s the neighbourhood has suffered from a low standard of housing and from the out-migration of middle-class families. Rates of dependency on public subsidies are particularly high among the families who are living in this area, while the average of the school certificates achieved by pupils and students resident in this area are lower than that of the city. In this context, the intention of the community centre is to promote self-organization and inter-cultural exchange between the diverse ethnic and age groups living in the neighbourhood.

A youth club and a youth association were established as early as 1984 in order to offer young people a centre for leisure time including cultural activities such as music and drama and for providing support for young people on a wide variety of issues that concern them (e.g. school, apprenticeships, career, police, parents, friends, partnerships). Five years ago, this youth work received a significant boost when the German Ministry for Family, the Elderly, Women and Youth granted three-years of funding in order to establish a youth drop-in centre which meant youth work activities could be extended substantially. Although the centre is open to all young people who seek advice, the main target group are young men and women between 14 and 22 years of age. The majority of these young people's families have immigrated from Turkey and Italy within the last two decades, but there are also many youngsters with their own unique migration histories. As you might expect the project is very much concerned with young people's transitions and the services it provides include individual counselling and the organization of home-work groups. The main focus of the empirical work was a drama group located in this centre. The drama group was initiated by an actress and drama teacher of Italian origin and the participants of the drama group are mainly young men from the local neighbourhood.

The target group and the objectives of the project Most of the participants have passed through the lowest level of the German school system. Half of them left compulsory education without any qualifications. Of those participating in the first group interview, three were unemployed with no prospect of training or schooling ahead. The majority though, have participated in youth training schemes for disadvantaged young people which lead to either to a training or school certificate, but which provide little in the way of genuine labour market prospects. When interviewed, they laughed off any suggestion that a career was a realistic goal for them. When asked if they had a dream job, a particularly telling reply was 'if we get one at all, that one will be our dream job' (group discussion 1).

As a means of illustrating the life-situation of the participants two illustrative portraits are presented here.

Portrait 1: Roberto Roberto was born in Italy 23 years ago. His family moved to Germany when he was three years old. He entered school at the age of six, but it soon became evident that he could not follow the classes properly due to his difficulties with the German language. He was transferred to the 'Special School' for pupils with learning difficulties from which he graduated at the age of 16, but with no certificate. Because he was unable to find an apprenticeship he then went on to the vocational preparation course. After the course he applied for many apprenticeships again but did not get any offers. He got into another vocational training scheme which he left after a few weeks because 'it did not lead anywhere'. Since then, he has worked in a greengrocer's from time to time. In 1999, he started a vocational training as an old people's nurse.

Portrait 2: Cengiz Cengiz was born in Mannheim in 1980. His parents had immigrated from Adana, Turkey two years prior to that. After Elementary School he proceeded to Hauptschule, the lowest level of secondary education. During the eighth term he had to leave school because of disciplinary problems. Because he had not finished the compulsory schooling time of nine years, he was then obliged to join a vocational preparation course. There he managed to get the lower secondary certificate and entered into an apprenticeship to be a plumber. While this part of the apprenticeship was a success, he had considerable difficulties with the teachers at the vocational school to the extent that he eventually dropped out. Since that time, he has combined short periods of work with times claiming Job Seeker Allowance.

By resuming his school career, he says 'I never did anything but sh*t at school, I simply did not know how to learn'. This changed when he was attending the vocational preparation course, because 'there everything was very easy, I was doing alright there'.

Both respondents have never participated in drama before they joined the drama group at the community centre.

Teaching Methods The drama group is organized on a group basis with two 3 hour meetings a week. The performing arts workshops are based on a variety of methodologies: the methods range from the forum theatre and others adopted from Augusto Boal's 'Theatre of the Oppressed' to elements of the classical Commedia dell'Arte. Boal's approach to teaching drama is based on his experiences as an actor and director under the Brazilian regime of the 1960s. During his work as a playwright and theatre director he has developed a set of methods which use drama as a weapon to fight any kind of oppression by building up the participants consciousness about their oppression and by giving them the tools to develop strategies of resistance. Boal was forced to emigrate to Argentine, Peru and, finally, came to

Europe where he continued to develop this approach. With oppressive
structures being more subtle in Europe as compared to Brazil, his approach
was adapted to the European situation. This has lead to a shift from a political to a more pedagogical and sometimes therapeutic stance in Boal's work:
'Politics are the therapy of the society and therapy is the politics of the individual' (interview with Boal, quoted in Neuroth,1994, p. 69). The main
appeal of Boal's approach, however, has remained the same: individuals
learn to see themselves as a part of societal structures. The aim of performing is to move towards change, as both an individual and as a group of
people in a similar situation.

There are other influences in the workshop leaders work which are as
important as the reference to Boal, but the most important element is the
common development of the performances out of 'generative themes'; that
is, the issues and concerns derived immediately from the learners everyday
life which provide starting points for the development of plots.

• Phase 1: Animation
In this 4 weeks phase students learn basic performance skills such as: concentration, relaxation, movement, breathing techniques and body language.
• Phase 2: Improvization
The second phase of 6 to 8 weeks consists of voice and mime exercises
which are performed individually and then in the form of group improvizations. The themes of the improvizations are set through negotiation between
the workshop leader and the participants.
• Phase 3: Production
Single scenes are developed from participants' ideas at this stage. A collage
of scenes is prepared for public performance. The duration of this phase is
decided by the group as a whole.

While the workshop leader stresses the importance of the group process
as the main objective of the work, the participants develop an orientation
towards a common goal: they learn to define their goals as a group and
generally aim to produce a public performance.

Young peoples' perceptions and access to the project The way in which
participants perceive the project is well illustrated by the following quota-
tion. When I asked the participants how and why they joined the project
one respondent replied:

'Yeah, you know it was winter and it was cold out there. We were meeting here with the boys anyway around the community centre, and one day we said why not give it a try and play drama.' (male, age 20)

In the following interviews this point was touched upon several times and the project appealed to the young people concerned in a variety of ways. Respondents often stressed the importance of the informal atmosphere during workshop sessions which were deemed to be far superior to the more formal atmosphere respondents associated with other institutional settings like vocational preparation courses, or school:

'Here we laugh a lot, we don't have to be serious **all the time**.' (male, age 18)

Informality also resulted from the peer group context in which the drama group was embedded: the participants stressed the fact that they all knew each other before the course, some of them having been friends for a long time.

In the one-to-one interviews, respondents emphasized the relationship between the course leader and the participants:

'She is more like a mate: you meet her and it's alright.' (male, age 17)

'Sometimes we need a little pressure, you see, but she is more like a sister to us.' (male, age 19)

This point was further underlined by the respondents on another occasion, when the group were asked what they would change in the drama group if they could:

'I would not change that much. We already decide a lot of things on our own: who can be part of the group, when do we take a weekend off for rehearsal, when do we want to perform before an audience.' (male, age 20)

The young people concerned were especially complimentary about the availability of professional advice,

'And sometimes I come here to talk to Siggi [the counsellor at the drop-in centre] for example when I have **trouble at home**.' (male, age 17)

The most striking thing about these observations is that the drama group is contrasted implicitly with previous or ongoing experiences with education and training institutions.

Career-related direct benefits An important concern of this research resides in the long-term career benefits of the project as perceived by the young people themselves. During a group interview a long discussion between the participants arose when one of them claimed that it would be good to include the drama group on his curriculum vitae.

> 'At the interview I had for my apprenticeship the interviewer asked me about it. He found it very interesting that I was doing drama.' (male, age 20)

Although some of the other boys were sceptical that membership of a drama group would have a significant impact on employers, most of them agreed that at least this would be a counterweight to the first impression the employers usually have when they face young men 'looking like us'.

> 'At least, if you tell them that you're in a drama group, they are likely not to think 'what is he doing all day long, he might be one of those drug-selling Turkish boys hanging around all day long.' (male, age 19)

Erol's case is an example of how some of the participants' aspirations grew more realistic during the course: Erol was already a break-dancer and rapper prior to joining the group. In his first one-to-one interview he has a clear goal. He wants to leave school as soon as possible to become a professional singer and dancer. As a mid-term objective he aspires to being a pop star. The course gave him the opportunity to pursue this goal by honing his performance skills. He is nonetheless convinced that he has to finish secondary school first (It is worth noting that in one interview the workshop leader told me that her greatest concern was to dissuade Erol from leaving school in his final year because he had recently been invited by a Turkish music company for a test recording in Istanbul and now feels he has a realistic chance of getting into the music business).

Learning effects In considering the learning effects of this course, a further question to be addressed is how participants perceive the learning processes and the personal benefits they have got from their participation in the course. While they reject the notion of 'work' to describe what they are doing, 'learning' seemed more appropriate to them. They see the drama workshop as a learning experience. As one of the participants put it, 'concentration is the main thing you learn here. Before the course started I could never concentrate on one thing, I always thought of a thousand things at a time. But now, I have learned how to concentrate. You will see, when you see us perform.' (male, age 23)

Performing for them is a means to get a message across to their audience. The message is mainly about what it means to live in Germany as a young migrant with next to no job prospects. Participants develop their plays out of improvizations which are all set in their own everyday lives. 'You can do anything you want on stage. Then you see, normal situations in the street, they could be like this, but on stage they can be different' (male, age 19). Thus, the group builds upon the foundation of 'naturalistic' issues to which the participants can actively relate. One such example is a scene set in the local employment office. The group take on the roles of: the young man looking for a job and the officer who tries to give him some advice and who by doing so discourages him. The young man is angry and disappointed. All the ingredients of this scene derive from the participants' own experiences and their interpretations of those experiences. The performances that the group develops pick up a wide range of concerns of individual members and not least the different expectations forced upon them by their families, their relationship with their friends, jobs, girlfriends, drugs, and attitudes towards violence. As one interviewee put it the main learning effect is: 'Seeing yourself from another perspective, and you see, yeah, it could be different' (male, age 20). Beyond these directly reported benefits, it is also possible to identify those secondary learning effects which may not be as immediately recognizable to the young people themselves.

Personal skills The central benefit, certainly in the opinion of the workshop leader is self-confidence. The drama group supplies the participants with opportunities to express themselves and to be creative and successful in contrast to other educational settings which tend to dwell on their inadequacies. Consider the example of one of the participants who appears to be quiet and marginalized from his peer group. He himself puts it this way:

'In school I was very quiet. When a teacher asked me a question I did not dare to answer.' (male, age 23)

In the one-to-one interview he was asked whether it was difficult for him to perform on stage. He answered:

'No, for the drama it is completely different. There you can act out your imagination.' (male, age 23)

The same young man summarizes the benefits to be had from his participation in the drama group:

'I know now how to concentrate. For example, in difficult situations like in the interviews I had with employers, I know now how to cope with this kind of situation. I think of what I want to say before I go into such situations. I no longer find it difficult to talk in front of many people. I am much more relaxed than I was before I started here.' (male, age 23)

An equally important learning effect is that of language as a means of expression. For most of the participants German is not their first language. In their everyday lives, with peers and family they either use the language of their parents (Turkish or Italian) or a German dialect which is a particular form of German blended with some aspects of Turkish and Italian. Neither of the latter two is recognized as an official language. By taking up the two of them as a productive and creative means of expressing oneself, the drama group gives real worth to these forms of speaking. On the other hand side, the drama group provides an opportunity for the participants to experiment without fear of retribution with 'proper German', the dominant everyday German spoken in schools and in other formal contexts. The workshop rehearsals appropriate mainstream German, but often use such language in a humorous fashion. In this way, the difficulties participants have in assimilating to the dialect and the dominant culture in general, are tackled in a way which prevents them from being labelled as deficient. Language can be used as a tool to demonstrate their underprivileged status, but playing with that language and using the power relationships it engenders as a springboard for humour, not only has hilarious consequences, but also provides a useful and powerful coping strategy, with the side-effect of increasing ease in their use of the German language.

The drama teacher prefers to emphasize the way in which drama helps participants to concentrate to learn about team-work. In her opinion, drama is all about constructing an identity: learning about who you want to be. This suggestion is reinforced by one of the participants who points out that,

'When you are acting you have to dive into it completely, you have to forget everything around you. That leads you to yourself, it brings you out of yourself.' (male, age 19)

Taking part in drama also seems to fulfil the participants' desire for quick positive feedback,

> 'You don't need to be perfect to see yeah that's great people have fun when they see me perform. In the beginning we thought we were great, but now we can see we knew nothing and we were bad, we have gotten better, but we can only see it now.' (male, age 20)

Not only does drama provide the sort of 'quick fix' that appeals to young people, it can provides them with a set of skills that are easily socially affirmed. Such affirmation contributes to the young men's feeling of self-efficacy and in turn breeds personal motivation.

Biographical skills The drama group gives the participants the opportunity to reflect upon their biographical situation in a way other learning settings cannot. By using their own ethnic background and youth culture as a positive platform upon which to develop ideas and by making this the starting point of the 'curriculum', participants can learn from their own circumstances without making those circumstances self-consciously therapeutic. This is an important point because the participants' resistance to any kind of intentional 'education' is one of the key characteristics of their educational biographies.

These young people are not 'trained' in personal skills like self-reflection. Such skills emerge as a side-effect of the drama work without being a threat or without pointing to the deficiencies in their own lives. And the participants do recognize this as the following young person illustrates:

> 'On stage you can be anything, you can try out and you see, yeah it could be different.' (male, age 17)

In this statement, we can also find the key to what Alheit describes as being the core aspect of biography construction: the ability to see oneself between the constraints of societal structures and our own subjectivity, and the ability to make sense out of this without losing the feeling of being in control of the circumstances in which you find yourself. One prerequisite of this key qualification (Alheit, 1995) is the potential for imagining where you might be in the future. One scene in the first play developed by the group provides a good example of how this works in practice. The participants perform a scene about a Sicilian family tragedy which graphically illustrates the direct confrontation between traditional and modern expectations and norms.

Social competencies and empowerment The workshop leader constantly stressed the importance of the group process as a major tool for providing many different learning opportunities. Participants' commitment to the drama group facilitated the development of their ability:

- to keep appointments and stick to agreements;
- to deal with group dynamics and conflicts – even in pressure situations such as when the deadline of a public performances approaches;
- to take group responsibility for common goals;
- and to negotiate the pace and the aspirations of the group.

In the above context, the development of group dynamics is particularly important:

> 'Learning to concentrate is important for my life. I know now how to deal
> with when the boys tell me do this don't do that. I just concentrate on what
> I want to do.' (group discussion 2)

In this statement, the respondent refers to the ability to reflect upon group norms and how he has gained the confidence and the communicative skills to resist inappropriate forms of peer pressure.

The promotion and development of the counselling infrastructure is one of the explicitly named objectives of the youth drop-in centre and as such the breakdown in communication between professional counsellors and young people represents one of the key the themes of the performances. As part of its work the group develops scenarios which often focus on power imbalances between adults and young people. This can be illustrated by one particular scene which the young people concerned had been developing since they first came together as a group.

The scene is concerned with vocational guidance at the Employment Service. In the German setting every student of lower secondary has to attend the counselling at least once at the end of his or her school career. Indeed, Employment Service officials are proud of the fact that the Berufsberatung (literally 'vocational counselling') 'reaches about one hundred per cent of school-leavers' (see Pohl 1997).

In the latest version of the sketch, to begin with the counsellor is displayed as a somewhat moody bureaucratic who only cares about how to keep his office furniture clean and safe from the young people who enter to seek advice. Before the visitors enter, he tests the distance between the visitor's chair and his own desk to make sure the visitor cannot touch the desk.

He always has a bottle of disinfectant handy on his desk to clean the things visitors have touched once they have left.

The counselling process itself is shown as a battle of wits between several advice-seeking young people and the counsellor. The goal as far as the young people is concerned is to get some information about jobs. In contrast, the counsellor is determined to find any available pretext as to why that individual should not get that information he or she requires, whilst instead ensuring that that they get signed up to a course they did not want anything to do with in the first place. The 'weapons' used in these battles include a variety of communication styles (speeches responded to by insults, aggression answered by aggression etc.). At the end of the scene, a smart young man enters the office and cleverly manages to get hold of the file of employment opportunities: he talks very politely to the officer and in the course of the conversation, the fact emerges that the officer hates his job. The youngster and the officer finally agree to switch their roles: the officer goes away happily to live without work and the boy takes over the officers 'fortune'; his collection of employment offers and his 'castle'; the desk.

In this hilarious and exaggerated form the actors bring to life on stage aspects of their own experiences with the Employment Service. The scene can certainly be interpreted as a means of asserting young masculine identities, but above all the scene and the process by which that scene is put together is an empowering one:

- the socio-cognitive aspect is the most obvious: the young men re-play a real-life experience, and usurp the power relationships they normally associate with that experience.
- communication is also important here. The different forms of verbal and non-verbal 'fight' for power between the two counterparts in each part of the sketches require a tremendous insight into the nuances of communication. The level of communication craftsmanship reached in this scene is, indeed, extraordinary.
- last, but not least, acting out an oppressive situation such as that described above culminates in a collective coping strategy (see Boal, 1982).

It is very important to these young people that their performances get public attention. In a public performance they have the opportunity to present themselves in a positive light in such a way that challenges dominant stereotypes. A useful illustration of the empowering nature of public performance is a theatre festival for students which is organized every year by

Mannheim's state-financed public theatre. A jury of professional actors and drama teachers select the best plays to be performed from the huge number that are submitted for consideration. Significantly, the JUST drama group submitted the only non-Gymnasium (the highest level secondary education in Germany) entry. The group's performance at the festival was an outstanding success. The regional newspapers spoke of the 'sensation' of the festival when they commented on their performance.

Gaining such public attention represents an ideal opportunity for the group to fight against the prejudices young people of the second generation of immigrants continue to face. The members of the group were very proud of this achievement. But they were also concerned about what might happen in public panel discussion after the show. As it happened their experiences as part of the drama group put them in good stead. They developed an ideal coping strategy in this context by electing two members spokespersons of the group and inventing some ideas for jokes they could make. This way, the two took control of the situation, whilst convincing everybody in the audience with their straight-forward and amusing answers.

Discussion

In this section I want to summarize the benefits the participants get from their experiences of their drama group, whilst attempting to indicate the conditions that make such benefits possible. First of all, it is important to acknowledge, as was pointed out above, that the labour market benefits of such training are not entirely clear. There are several structural reasons for this. In Germany there is a large gap between the lower levels of secondary education and a career in performing arts. Professional actors are usually trained at specialized schools which are either, private and expensive, or are run by the state and therefore only admit students who have achieved a baccalaureat. The young people at JUST are therefore very unlikely to be able to pursue a professional acting career. Having said that, the media and entertainment sectors are rapidly growing sectors and in current economic circumstances a growing differentiation of the work force is undoubtedly required. Nonetheless, youth and community work are highly regulated labour markets with well-established and standardized vocational pathways. It is highly unlikely that people without Polytechnic or University degrees will be able to get a job in this field.

The important thing to remember here is that this project is not aiming to replace vocational training, nor to produce young people ready to enter the labour market. Rather, the project leader's see the performing arts as one part of what they call a 'holistic approach' to pre-vocational education and vocational guidance. Indeed, in 1998, the project was elected to serve as a pilot project for 'neighbourhood-based prevention of labour market exclusion' by the German Ministry for Labour. It therefore seems appropriate to sketch some options for future development where such projects could play an important role in the future of the transition system:

- There is vast potential for job creation within the culture industry which provides for a lot more jobs than just musicians, actors and dancers. It can also provide an attractively flexible careeer for young people who are often 'turned off' by more conventional career paths.
- Such projects may play an invaluable role in giving young people a fulfilling and interesting means of passing the time during times of un-employment. Such projects help young people to attain a form of cultural citizenship whilst helping to feel they belong in a society in which all sorts of other ways they do not.

The above ideas are far from exhaustive. But what they do illustrate is the fact that a more flexible and pragmatic view of the transition system can reap rewards. Innovative projects such as JUST can fill a gap in what tends to be a rather inflexible system. Many under-achieving young people are not motivated by the current system, not because they are incapable of be-ing motivated but because the system is too inflexible to cater to their needs. This research has illustrated that drama provides an especially effec-tive means of providing 'disadvantaged' young people with an arena for self-development which is not otherwise provided for them by the main-stream.

The British case study

The labour market situation

There is a strong argument for suggesting that young people in Britain have been affected more than any other sector by the ramifications of recent economic change and notably the decline in full-time employment and a growth in part-time and short-term forms of employment. De-industrialization and subsequent structural unemployment have, indeed, hit young people disproportionately hard, 'Obscuring paths to adult statuses, identities and activities'. (MacDonald, 1997, p. 186). Many commentators have pointed out that the relative position of under 25s in Britain actually worsened during the 1990s with the gap between the unemployment rate for all ages and that of the under 25s being greater in the 1990s than it was in the 1980s (Brinkley, 1997).

Those young people who do enter the job market are very likely to be concentrated into particular occupations. In England and Wales, for example, 68 per cent of 16 year old school leavers entered sales and personal and protective services, craft and related and clerical and secretarial occupations (YCS, 1996). In this context, Ashton and Maguire (1990) found that many young people's early careers were very likely to involve a series of shifts between government training schemes, semi and unskilled work and most worryingly, unemployment. In short, employment in general, and employment for young people in particular is especially insecure (see Robinson, 1997). Indeed, during the mid-late 1990s unemployment amongst 16 – 19 year olds remained at a steady 17.5 per cent, but rising from just over 10 per cent in 1989. However, it is worth remembering that since the withdrawal of unemployment benefits for under-18s young people who are not in education or training and are without work are not officially recognized as unemployed. What has emerged in this context is a culture of dependency where more and more financial and emotional strain is put on the family unit. In this context, a particular concern resides in what Williamson (1997) has described as the emergence of Status Zer0 youth, young people in their mid-teens who do not appear to participate in education, training and employment and who are therefore consigned to marginalized economic futures. Such developments reflect broader changes in unemployment and homelessness which have almost become common characteristics of youth transitions, creating a set of circumstances where young people are faced with a complex range of options which have to be confronted at a personal subjective level (Blackman, 1998; Furlong and Cartmel, 1997; Winefield *et al.* 1993). The seriousness of this situation is illustrated by the fact that whilst 608,000 16 to 17 year olds entered the job market in 1984/5, as few as 276,000 entered in 1992. Although such changes can be partially accounted for by developments in training and education, a large proportion of young people are not taking up the opportunities available to them. Many of those disaffected young people unaccounted for in these figures have 'fallen through the net', as the statutory services have struggled to respond to their particular set of social care requirements.

The current situation is such that by their mid-twenties most young people will have had some experience of unemployment. The British Birth Cohort study found that among young people unemployed at the age of 26, 90 per cent of men and 78 per cent of women had previously experienced substantial periods of unemployment. Bynner *et al.* (1997) argue that a key safeguard against prolonged unemployment are qualifications.

The structure of the British transition system

The majority of young people in Britain are educated as part of a comprehensive system which aims to accommodate young people of all abilities. There are, however, exceptions to this rule: for instance, a small minority of young people attend private fee-paying schools. There are also some variations between those structures in place in England and Wales and those in Scotland. Compulsory education begins in Britain at the age of 5. At the age of 11 a child will move from primary school to secondary school. He or she will more than likely leave secondary school at the end of the fifth year, at 16 years of age or at any stage after. As far as qualifications are concerned, students aim towards the achievement of General Certificate of Secondary Education (GCSE) awards for which they sit nationally accredited examinations and coursework. Having, in most cases, sat GCSE examinations students have three main choices, depending on the level of their previous academic achievements:

- Move into the sixth form to continue their studies;
- Choose to sign up on a vocational course in a Further Education College;
- Move into the labour market, either directly (through employment) or indirectly through a youth training programme.

Perhaps the most interesting aspect of recent transitions into adulthood is that more and more young people are pursuing their education, either through a traditional academic route or through alternative training programmes and less and less are going straight into the job market at the age of 16. This is not simply because there are more educational opportunities available but because of the fact, that, as many commentators have argued, young people represent the most vulnerable sector of the employment market (Roberts, 1995). Historically, levels of participation in upper secondary education in Britain have lagged behind many other European countries including Belgium, Denmark, France and Germany. Only 40 per cent of young people between the ages of 16 and 18 were in full-time education at the beginning of the 1990s compared to more than three quarters in the above countries (DfEE 1993). Since the late 1980s this pattern has radically altered. The proportion of those young people who remain in the upper secondary school for two further post-compulsory years has more than doubled between 1981 and 1993 from 18 to 44 per cent (SOEID, July 1996). As already indicated the collapse of the youth labour market in recent years is a primary factor in influencing a trend that appears on the surface to be purely positive. The government decision to remove any possibility of unemployment benefit prior to the age of 18 is also an important factor here, as is a general lack of confidence amongst young people in the training schemes themselves. Although as authors such as Furlong and Cartmel (1997) have noted there are clear class dimensions to these trends, even those pupils with below average attainment are increasingly likely to remain at school for a year or two extra (Paterson and Raffe, 1995).

In the above context, the effectiveness of conventional Youth Training programmes is a matter for considerable debate (Biggart and Furlong, 2000). There is a strong suspicion that Youth Training fails to capture the imagination of those young people who partake in it. There is also a grave concern amongst those involved in youth work that such schemes are intended to offset youth unemployment rather than provide young people with the skills they actually need. In recent years efforts have been made to address this problem and, in particular, to raise the skill content of such training, whilst addressing the exploitative reputation of such schemes. The problem often appears to be related to the question of motivation. Young people quite often feel that they are little more than slave labour that they are being exploited for a minuscule wage in a 'job' that teaches them very little of long term value (see Banks *et al.* 1992). In other words, they fulfil a role in their place of training, but the limited skills they gain are of very limited value beyond the specific workplace in which those skills were learnt. Authors such as Banks *et al.* (1992) have conducted research which illustrates that young people are dissatisfied with training if it fails to lead directly to a job and often it does not. Roberts (1995) points out that few trainees found that the experience and qualifications gained on the scheme were of any advantage in the wider labour market. There is, indeed, an underlying feeling that at least some training involves 'parking' young people without them gaining improved working prospects. As such, 'Motivation to train currently runs on motivation to work, whereas education can be seen as an end in itself.' (Banks et al, p. 46) Some recent developments in training provision such as the introduction of Youth Credits appear to have helped address the problem of demotivation, but the problem of low pay and patronizing treatment on the part of work-based trainers remains an enormous one. Of equal concern is evidence that training schemes are highly stratified. Members of ethnic minorities, for example, are far more likely to be concentrated in schemes with the worst record of employment take-up (Roberts, 1995). Such schemes are also gender divided to the extent that young women are more likely to be trained in what is generally perceived to be 'women's' work. Meanwhile, Wilkinson (1995) argues that the main feeling amongst young people is that there simply is not enough choice available to young people who feel coerced into training they simply do not want to do. In short, 'It is crucial that training schemes have a real purpose, that they provide relevant skills and will provide a real opportunity for young people to move to employment.' (L. Van-Waterschoot, 1998). It still remains to be seen whether the New Deal, a programme which is intended to help 250,000 18 – 25 year olds back into work and which was introduced in Britain in 1998 can actively address this problem. This programme officially removes the option of being unemployed and gives young people five options: employment for six months including one day a week training; full time education and training; voluntary sector employment and a place on an environmental task force or self-employment. Additional schemes including the vocationally based New Start which is aimed at 14 – 19 year olds who have dropped out of education, learning or employment have also been introduced to this end. The success of such schemes depends on a wide variety of factors. But perhaps, of most concern is the extent to which young people are being offered skills and opportunities that both motivate them and provide them something they can use in the workplace.

It is for the above reasons that less traditional training schemes are so fascinating. There is a strong feeling in the literature that a successful training scheme is directly related to the opportunity to work afterwards. The New Deal has at least begun to recognize the fact that less conventional schemes can tap into young people's imaginations, give them self-belief and hope for the future. Perhaps in a climate in which employers continue to be more impressed by academic qualifications than vocational training, the funding devoted to youth training is insufficient. Ultimately, young people themselves are the ambassadors of these programmes. A detailed discussion of the training provided by Hope Street may well illustrate the benefits of training, not for training's sake, but for the sake of the young people who partake in such training.

The Hope Street project

Liverpool, located in the county of Merseyside is an industrial city of just over 450, 000 inhabitants. Similar to Mannheim, Liverpool has struggled to deals with the problems associated with de-industrialization and has one of the worst unemployment rates in the UK. By the 1990s economic development in Merseyside fell below the EU average and as a result Merseyside

was granted Objective 1 status in 1993. 55 per cent of the Liverpool population live in 'Pathways Areas', those areas experiencing the poorest
economic and social conditions in the county. Despite some recent im-
provements in local economic performance and a fall of 44 per cent in the
unemployment rate between 1986 and 1996, Liverpool's unemployment
still stands at twice that of the national average at around 15 per cent. In
August 1996 46.2 per cent of those unemployed had been out of work for
more than one year compared with 35.5 per cent nationally, and 13 per cent
(around twice the national average) had been unemployed for more than 5
years. In addition to long term unemployment there is also a high incidence
of unemployment among the under 25s and almost a third of the total fall
into the category compared with 27.7 per cent for Great Britain (see
http://ds.dial.pipex.com/liv.cpu/cspr/needs.htm).

Project description and target group Hope Street is a training organization
based in the heart of Liverpool, Merseyside which offers arts training for
young people. Hope Street was originally set up in 1989 as a partnership
between Liverpool City Council and the Everyman Theatre who with the
help of the Liverpool City Education Department and European funding
decided to set up and run programmes aimed, primarily at unemployed
young people. This is reflected in the fact that Liverpool, which is located
in the industrial north west, remains one of the most deprived areas in the
country. Indeed, the fact that Liverpool was recently 'awarded' Objective
One Status for seven additional years indicates that it remains one of the
poorest regions in Europe. The following comments from one of the directors of Hope Street illustrates the sorts of difficulties young people are
experiencing,

> 'Liverpool used to be on top of the football league and we were top of the
> league of music as well, and now we're top of the league for
> unemployment... And every time you get statistics its like Liverpool have
> gone from whatever 20 per cent to 15 per cent, oh that's good! The national
> average is 5 per cent unemployment. What people cannot understand is that
> it is not a stigma anymore, it's like its a lifestyle now, because its been
> apparent for so long and its in generations. What that disguises is how
> corrosive it is, but its a common problem of young people, unemployment
> you know. And its being employed in something you want to do, that is
> challenging, that is worthwhile, that you value.'

Economic decline has hit young people especially badly in this regard. In
this context, young people appeared to **have even less** chance of securing

employment, and even less so career-oriented employment, than suggested by the national picture.

Initially, the development of Hope Street was very much bound up with broader priorities of the Everyman theatre. Having said that the particular ethos of Hope Street was beginning to emerge. The early days of Hope Street and of 'Acting Up' in particular were remarkable insofar it was the only type of training incorporating a bias towards unemployed excluded people in the country that was tied to a mainstream theatre. However, the relationship between the actual theatre and Hope Street eventually disbanded, as the Directors of Hope Street took on a more independent role. 'Acting Up' emerged as a pre-vocational performing arts course accredited by the Merseyside Open College Federation and open to disadvantaged young people aged 16-25. The course ran over a period of nine months and, on the surface at least, offered young people practical experience and training in drama and music. Young people joining the course were unemployed, but generally had some degree of interest in the performing arts. 'Acting Up' was very practical and in some ways informal in nature with the main emphasis being on engendering those skills necessary for the preparation of a public performance. However, the Directors of Hope Street are not embarrassed to draw attention to their courses as courses in social education, as well as in music and drama. Even Hope Street's advertising points out the organization's intention to

'provide social and personal development for disadvantaged young people in order to improve their confidence and self-esteem which in turn can help them become more aware of opportunities and make informed choices about their lives.'

Herein lies the underlying philosophy of Acting Up and of Hope Street in general.

The intention of Hope Street is to use the performing arts as a vehicle upon which the young unemployed can develop those communicative and confidence-based skills that are becoming more and more important in a de-structured labour market. 'Acting Up' therefore involved twenty five young 25 young people work together for nine months preparing performances. This process therefore involves thematic work and research on the issue of the show, writing song lyrics or improvising on the drama play, training in acting and music making, rehearsals and performance. In the second part of the course workshop leading skills became more of a priority and are delivered in schools, youth clubs and in the context of international exchange projects.

As central government policy has changed, so has Hope Street had to changed with it. Fortunately, the changes that have occurred have also very much fitted in to the underlying Hope Street philosophy. The New Deal and the investment in Hope Street that the New Deal brings is such that Hope Street have to be very transparent about the aims of their training programmes which have now taken on a different guise. Although at first the staff at Hope Street appeared to be somewhat wary of the impact of the New Deal, they have become increasingly open to its potential benefits. Indeed, the director of the organization actually said that the 'New Deal' could have been a disaster or a saviour for Hope Street. Fortunately, in his opinion it was the latter. The people running Hope Street had certain ideas about how the training they offered should develop and were particularly concerned that the outcomes of such training, in terms of what it actually did for young people, should be more focused. 'Acting Up' has, in effect, been replaced by a 'Workshop Leaders' programme which although broadly speaking works on the same basis as its predecessor, is in some ways more vocationally focussed in nature. This a 26 week programme, the first six weeks of which involves developing a variety of performance based skills to do with group-work, teaching and performance in general. During the first six weeks the young people concerned will go out on informal placements to community groups in order to get to know the people they will actually train themselves in the remainder of the course. A group of two or three young people will then join the community group concerned for a full six weeks, during which time they will put together a performance. A free lance worker employed by Hope Street will at this time be on hand to help where necessary. However, should there be no problems, then the said freelancer would withdraw and allow the young people training to continue their good work. At the end of that six weeks having completed a performance, and having analysed how things may have been done differently the group move on to a larger community project. In 2000 for instance, Hope Street worked with a special needs school with 120 children who were introduced to the benefits of drama. Having completed that part of the training the young people return to Hope Street to receive further vocational guidance and to construct a portfolio outlining the experiences and the skills they had learnt. The tone of the training delivered by Hope Street appears to have changed. It is certainly more applied in nature and it is perhaps guided more by vocational imperatives than was previously the case. The positive benefit of such a change in tone is that this training is lead even more by the needs of the community where, after all, young people are most likely to get the jobs they aspire to. The nature of this change is further reinforced by a recent addition to Hope Street's training portfolio, the 'Transition to Work' programme. This is a European funded initiative that gives young people actual work experience in delivering drama-based workshops in the local community. The programme is educational and seeks to inform children of a variety of ages about sex education or 'Healthy Living' in an entertaining way that relates to their everyday lives.

Most young people attending Hope Street have passed through the lowest level of the UK school system. Having left school with few if any qualifications many of those interviewed had never had a job. Many therefore participated in a variety of youth training schemes, attendance at which might almost be said to have become a youth culture in its own right. In order to illustrate the biographies of the sorts of young people attending Hope Street I will now present two portraits.

Portrait 1: Darren Darren is 19 years old. He says he hated school and tended to avoid attending as much as possible. He describes the school he went to as a 'dump'. Managing to finish school with a single qualification and a low grade at that, Darren spent the next 6 months 'playing video games' and 'watching day-time TV', until one day his mother showed him an advertisement about Hope Street in the local newspaper. Darren had always fancied himself as a bit of a show-off but had never really though of a career in performance. Actually, he was quite happy to stay at home doing his own thing, but his mum persuaded him that Hope Street might be a good idea. He says 'it was the best thing I've ever done' and eventually hopes to get a job as an actor.

Portrait 2: Carole Carole is 21 years old. She was brought up in Liverpool and has lived there her entire life. She was never very successful at school and eventually left at 16 with no qualifications. Uncertain what she might do having left school, Carole filled in with a few part-time menial jobs. But she always had an interest in the Arts and in performance and eventually got a place at a local college, Greenbank. Having completed this particular course she spotted a newspaper advertisement for 'the 'Workshop Leaders Course' which she completed successfully, so much so that she was invited to participate in the 'Transition to Work' programme which she is currently working on.

The intention of this project is to identify what benefits lie in a community-arts based programme and how the skills young people gain from their experiences in Hope Street, in particular, might vary from more traditional forms of training. Perhaps the first and most important point to make reflects the underlying philosophy of Hope Street, as discussed in an interview with one of the organization's **directors**, who is keen to move away from a culture which has a tendency to blame young people for the disadvantages they apparently experience. He therefore pointed out that one of the primary tasks of his staff was to encourage young people to recognize that the fact they are unemployed,

> '...is nothing to do with you why you are in this situation. It's to do with where you were born; the school. It's nothing to do with you, so you can easily turn that corner.'

Hope Street is therefore all about hope; about encouraging young people that they can aspire to a career and that they have got something to offer. On one level then, Hope Street is concerned wit providing the foundations upon which young people can get jobs. But the point here, is that they realize that they are capable of doing, not any old job, but an actual career which can fulfil them. In short, Hope Street's philosophy is not about simply providing the foundations upon which young people can get a job and a wage which gets them off the street, but about providing them with the skills and the confidence that they can do jobs that they *want* to do. The people who run Hope Street are very concerned that their organization is not entirely controlled by central government. They feel strongly that an independent agenda is important if Hope Street is able to provide young people with training they can use. In this sense Hope Street says just as much about the imagination and commitment of its founders than that of the young people it supports. The award of a grade one from the Training Standards Council is testament to how successful Hope Street continues to be in balancing the demands of a broader educational agenda with the needs of young people. The programmes on offer here offer young people a plethora of skills and not simply those skills we would associate with the arts. The investment made by the New Deal and by other sources of funding, is not an investment in the organization itself or even in the building in which such young people are centred, but an investment in young people. All monies are ploughed back into training provision. The director I interviewed estimated that in this context only about 10 per cent of those young people trained at Hope Street actually get a job in the performing arts. This may not appear to be a very high proportion, but as interviews with the young people undertaking such training will indicate, the aim of Hope Street is not to provide direct entry into the performing arts, but rather to provide experiences and the motivation according to which young people can begin to believe in themselves.

Drama as a vehicle for training Given the above, drama and performance should be regarded as a vehicle for training rather than an end itself. Many of those interviews commented on how drama in particular allows young people a unique opportunity to learn new skills. Above all, perhaps, drama allows young people to put to one side some of those reservations and uncertainties that are so synonymous with growing up. As one respondent put it, drama gives young people the opportunity to be idiotic without fear of reprisals. It provides a space where young people are free to make mistakes. Young people spend a considerable amount of time worrying about what other people think of them. As several respondents pointed out, drama allows for a degree of escape. It allows young people to express emotions and feelings that would not normally be allowed because it constructs a blind between themselves and the people around them. It provides a legitimate context within young people can explore themselves,

'It's not just about getting a performance. The performance at the end of the day is one thing, but the process is so much more important... It's all about enjoying it and really getting something out of it.' (female, age 20)

Performance therefore provides a self-motivating vehicle which young people actually enjoy. The danger is that youth training more often reflects the needs of the economy and of the providers of that training than it does the needs of young people themselves. As a result, young people tend to be under-motivated and do not manage to get very much out of the training they do receive, simply because they do not enjoy it and it does not constitute a genuine challenge. Many of my respondents discussed the differences between the course provided at Hope Street and others they had experienced. Many discussed courses that offered drama as a vehicle, but were also driven by theory rather than practice. This reinforces the point that courses like 'Acting Up' and 'Workshop Leaders' are not simply about training young people to be performers. They do not, for instance, provide the theoretical foundations that many commentators would argue are necessary for a professional acting career. On the other hand, such courses do provide the hands-on experience which helps to make young people the authors of their own training. In some senses then young people felt they had more freedom at Hope Street. Hope Street meant a lot to many of my respondents insofar as it had a particular atmosphere; an atmosphere that appreciated young people on the courses as individuals, rather than as units there to make up the numbers,

'I think with the course I was on before I wasn't really noticed. I felt like they barely knew my name. At Hope Street they did. And they could recognize my talents as well. If you had talent they'd push 'yer. They'd go,

'you're good at this, you should do this or that's your responsibility...'
(male, age 21)

In contrast, other more traditional courses tend to be rather impersonal in
nature. The small scale of Hope Street provides a context in which one-to-
advice becomes a reality, and within which the individual's career, as opposed to the need to complete the programme of training become the key
focus of attention. In this context, one or two respondents commented how
they were particularly impressed by the fact that the people in charge at
Hope Street, allowed young people a voice. In other words, young people
were not simply the object of the training. Any ideas or suggestions they
had about how such training could be improved are borne in mind. One of
the directors of Hope Street provided more of an overview of the current
state of youth training in Britain when he suggested that far too many training courses are predictable in nature, 'doing little more than paying the
wages of those running the courses'. There is from this point of view, a
genuine concern that the majority of current training programmes suffer
from a basic lack of quality; that they simply are not addressing young
people's actual training needs.

The aims of Hope Street In order to consider the success of Hope Street in
providing a form of training that meets young people's training needs
whilst also motivating them into a mindset in which a career becomes a
genuine possibility, it is important to discuss the aims of course such as
'Acting Up' and 'Workshop Leaders' as articulated by the leaders of the
course and those on the course.

   An interview with one of the director's of Hope Street indicated that in
the present climate the need to get a job and to provide the sort of training
that will qualify young people for a job is paramount. In a sense, Hope
Street provides an environment in which young people experience some of
the discipline associated with work, in terms of having to turn up at desig-
nated times and having to work in conjunction with a group of others,
whilst making the young people concerned more employable in the process.
The project director therefore listed the sorts of objectives and skill acquisition that underpinned the Hope Street experience:

- How to negotiate with others;
- How to work in a team;
- Reaching deadlines;
- How to research;
- Working independently and part of a group;

- Being confident about autonomous decision-making;
- Being honest and open about making mistakes;
- Being committed to the project;
- Discipline and time-keeping;
- The ability to listen;
- Basic report writing skills, presenting information and yourself in a favourable light;
- Communication skills;
- Confidence.

The above list is by no means exhaustive, but it is worth noting that none of the above points could be an exclusive preserve of the performing arts. The intention is not solely to teach young people how to perform, but to teach them some of the generic skills that emerge from the ability to plan and stage a performance.

As far as the interview with the project director is concerned, the community-based nature of the project soon became clear. At one point he described what Hope Street offered as a 'community work' course. In effect, young people are encouraged through the doors of Hope Street by the surface appeal and glamour of performance. If the courses Hope Street provides were advertized as 'social education' they simply would not appeal. Having arrived at Hope Street, the project emphasizes the links between performance and the local community. Young people are encouraged to give something back, through performance, to their locality. In this sense the training young people receive at Hope Street is not individualized, but is a product of community participation. In addition, the sorts of skills I described above are equally applicable in youth clubs, play centres, and elderly people's homes and these are the sorts of locations that many of those attending Hope Street will end up working in. The director suggested Hope Street was creating an atmosphere within which social entrepreneurship becomes the norm. The 'Healthy Living' programme for instance, is very much concerned with delivering placements in the community from which offers of short-term work are often forthcoming. The impact of the New Deal has meant that youth training clearly has an economic dimension to it. Young people need to be trained in ways in which they can serve the economy, but this should not rule out the possibility that such training can also have a positive social benefit. Many young people are simply not motivated by the prospect of a 9 to 5 job, but they are motivated by the prospect of gaining fulfilling employment. Hope Street encourages them to be open to the possibilities of a work mentality. The introduction of such a mentality in a region in which unemployment tends to be the norm amongst young people represents an enormous responsibility for Hope Street which has had to become increasingly professional as a result, as the director pointed out,

> 'We're changing young people's lives. And I used to be very embarrassed about saying that, but I think we're actually very professional at changing young people's lives, rather than being informal. I think we're less friendly on the surface and we're more committed and more professional and I think therefore the people that come through our door get a better service.'

The perceived intentions of Hope Street as indicated by one of its director's are perhaps surprisingly duplicated by both those young people on one of Hope Street's courses and those who have completed such a course. Many of those interviewed accepted that 'Acting Up' in particular, was not simply about learning drama, but was ultimately concerned with securing those skills necessary if a job is to be a realistic long-term prospect. There appears to be a general acceptance that although Hope Street cannot guarantee a job, it is geared to helping young people get jobs eventually. This may, for instance, involve helping young people become qualified so they can sign up to other courses. Some young people referred to Hope Street's hidden agenda; which has less to do with acting and performance and more to do with putting young people's foot on the first rung of the job ladder. According to the young people working at Hope Street, the place gives them a chance in a world that otherwise does not,

> 'It gives you a go this course [Acting Up]. We've all had a chance to have a go. Like when you go outside now to get a go, you will have a go. Before we might not of.' (male, age 18)

Acting Up and the Workshop Leader's course therefore appear to open people's minds to the possibilities that lie in front of them. Several young people remarked how it gave them valuable experience and the opportunity to express themselves in a creative arena which they actively enjoyed. The practical element of such courses represented a key attraction to the young people concerned, as was the freedom to use and apply original ideas in the context of a performance. Far from being constrained by the straight-jacket of a curriculum young people felt, at least to an extent, that they were able to use their own imaginations. Another key aim of 'Acting Up' according to my respondents was the opportunity it gave them to interact with a variety of different people from different backgrounds with different skills.

Some respondents therefore recognized and appreciated the social dimension of the course,

> 'I don't think 'Acting Up' is just a course on acting. Its a social course. It teaches you social skills. It teaches you how to communicate, to talk to people and the idea is that when you go to work you can sell yourself. It is all about holding yourself and believing in yourself.' (female, age 22)

Discussion

Hope Street provides an environment in which young people are given the space to find a new direction in life. As one young person suggested, whilst on 'Acting Up' or the 'Workshop Leaders' course, people might not actually realize the benefits to be had. But having completed the course the broader benefits beyond the confines of drama such as the ability to communicate, to listen, bearing in mind other people's needs and the need to present yourself in a favourable light, become ever clearer. As the director of Hope Street pointed out, when young people come to Hope Street they are no longer, black or white, unemployed or disadvantaged. They are themselves and the opportunity to be themselves is a rarity. Hope Street promotes a particular atmosphere which, above all, helps young people to feel that they belong and that they can pursue their own potential. The benefit of Hope Street then is to promote self-belief (which we will discuss in more detail shortly) but also as one young people indicated, 'To give the insight like there's another world outside Liverpool.' That world has two dimensions: one in which you as an individual are appreciated and in which you can express yourself and another in which the local community comes to life. As one respondent put it Hope Street opens people up to real life. This much was illustrated by the fact that Hope Street is open to people from a variety of personal backgrounds and in order to maintain this status quo Hope Street is run on a day-to-day basis according to a reasonably strict disciplinary code. A primary intention of this code is that Hope Street should be a safe space. It is in this respect that young people are also encouraged to respect all others regardless of their gender or ethnicity. Hope Street is very much founded on the desire to open people's minds to the realities of everyday life and to this end, to discourage racism and sexism.

The issue that came up time and time again in my interviews, however, was that of confidence. As one respondent put it, you may or may not have confidence before you arrive at Hope Street, but courses like 'Acting Up' channel such confidence in appropriate directions. It provides the context within which young people can explore their own potential, whilst developing such confidence. One respondent indeed suggested that Hope Street was *all* about confidence. It manages to 'open people up' and 'come out of themselves'. Many of these young people may not feel particularly good about themselves. Hope Street provides an environment which is open and accepting enough for people to take risks and be prepared to feel good about what they were doing. The young people I interviewed were proud of what Hope Street was all about and proud of their own individual roles in making a performance work. One respondent, for instance, recounted the occasion when a group of young people advertized the play they were performing by standing up in a pub as a group to rehearse a song in front of everybody. The same student talked about one particularly shy member of that group,

> 'See we had this lad on the first block of the course. He was really shy and never said anything to anybody. Very quiet. There was improvement in him: the rest of the group got behind him a lot. Help him with his voice. We dragged him along to the pub. He started to make excuses at first, but you could see he really wanted to go. He was a bit on his own. So eventually we insisted he came, almost carried him at one point to come out with us. Yeah, we brought him out of his shell eventually. That's another good thing about this place. Even if you don't want to be an actor maybe, if you're quiet and maybe you need more confidence this is somewhere to come. After that first block we couldn't shut this bloke up, he was really into it. Acting Up was brilliant for him.' (female, age 21)

Indeed, instances in which the confidence engendered in 'Acting Up' in particular are apparently endless. One such example occurred during a performance before which everybody had been extremely nervous. In order to lighten the atmosphere and as a means of lifting the morale of the group, one young person took the risk of improvising his character's lines. The rest of the cast followed suit and that particular performance was a great success. Hope Street provides the sort of atmosphere in which people can let go of their inhibitions. Having said that, it is worth remembering that there is a fine line between being confident and being unbearably arrogant. As the Hope Street director indicated it was the staff's job to ensure this line was not crossed. One of the key intentions of Hope Street was therefore to keep young people's feet on the ground and to ensure that every young person recognizes that their experience of Hope Street and of the performances they take part in whilst at Hope Street, only constitute one step along the way to success. But the main thing is that Hope Street does appear to be successful in giving young people the confidence to 'have a go' at pursuing their interests. As one respondent pointed out an interest in drama, may not lead to a career, but at least they have had a go at it, and at least they have been prepared to make mistakes along the way from which they can learn,

> 'Well, in a way its teaching you what skills you have and by doing that your empowering yourself because you're believing in yourself. I mean a lot of people left 'Acting Up' and they didn't want to do acting, but they got confidence. They got confidence to do what they want to do. They got to believe in themselves. And when we did it as well, because they were devised pieces we were given a lot of the responsibility and its like if its sh*t, its our ideas. So its 'Oh my God' all the time. So its like putting pressure on ourselves. We did because we wanted to and that was really good as well. I think it does give people that. It lets you sort of believe in yourself and it puts that pressure on you. And its just like 'I've produced this and I'm the one whose gotta stand on stage in front of the audience.' (female, age 22)

The young people I interviewed spoke in length about the benefits that Hope Street gave them in terms of boosting their confidence. But they also referred to a variety of other secondary learning effects and skills that they felt their time at Hope Street had given them. Particularly significant in this respect were group and team-building skills. Many of the young people I interviewed had not previously been exposed to the benefits and disciplines of group work. Many commented on how much they learnt in terms of listening to their fellow students and the teamwork that drama encapsulates was especially instructive to them, insofar as, in a sense, they became less self-centred as a result,

> 'When you are working in a team you have to keep your energy up 'cos if one person starts to sag the rest of the group starts to sag as well. So everybody's responsible for keeping their own energy up and that brings the team together. Someone struggles. Someone whose maybe had more experience steps in and helps them. That's happened a lot.' (male, age 19)

Several respondents commented that 'Acting Up' taught them respect and the trust that working in a team brings with it. The message was that acting is not simply about reading your script but it is about working with and being aware of other people and of giving and taking. One respondent told me about some of the exercises that were undertaken as part of Acting Up. One such exercise involved an individual running around and jumping and the remainder of the group applauding that person for doing just that. Another exercise was about complimenting every member of the group regardless of whether or not you got on with them as an individual. One student pointed out that a lot of people in the group found it difficult to accept compliments, perhaps because prior to Hope Street they had not really felt that they had been good at very much,

> 'It's like accepting that everybody has their good point and accepting your own, so if you do go out and get another job, you accept, alright, I might of done Acting Up but how did I use these skills. So alright I have organized things. I did communicate with people. I worked well as a team member and I also lead the team at certain points. So you've got all these skills you don't actually realize you've got.' (female, age 22)

One of the most important attributes of 'Acting Up' was therefore the way in which it helped individual's to see themselves as both belonging to a group and as having responsibility as part of that group. Amongst other things Hope Street also taught people to be patient, to listen and to take account of other people's needs and also how to solve problems. One young person talked about a typical scenario during the 'Workshop Leaders' programme when the group organized a workshop for ten people and only two people turn up, which meant their plans needed an immediate rethink: the sort of challenge the young people at Hope Street were confident enough to meet.

So what does all this add up to? What did the experience of Hope Street and the acquisition of the above skills and in particular do for the young people concerned? The data we collected seems to indicate, above all, that the training provided by Hope Street allowed young people to 'find' themselves. Whereas, according to our respondents, more conventional courses appeared to be going through the motions and providing training apparently for no other reason than to fill time, Hope Street goes far deeper than that,

> 'I don't think the course just gives confidence, it gives you whatever you're lacking. So if you can't shut up like in my case, then you learn to work with a group. If you're too quiet you learn to speak. You learn whatever. You learn to get the ability that you haven't got.' (male, age 20)

As a vehicle drama allowed young people to 'open themselves up'; to who they are as an individual, but also to the possibilities of the future. At the beginning of their time at Hope Street many of the young people I interviewed said they felt they were attending just another training course, but the course surprised them in the way it opened up their eyes to what they might do in the future. One young person described **Hope Street as giving** her the power and the confidence to go out there and find what she wanted to do: the belief that something could be done with her life. If Hope Street does one thing, it gives young people a chance in a climate in which they would generally get very few chances at all. In short, Hope Street gives young people the foundations upon which they can empower themselves,

> 'Do you know that person in the mirror when you're on yourself in the bedroom and you're singing with your brush in the mirror and you'd never do that in front of anyone. It brings that person out in yer' in the group. You don't have to pretend to anyone. It drags that person out of you.' (male, age 19)

The member of staff I interviewed echoed this feeling amongst the young people attending Hope Street. He pointed out that there are lots of clichés banded about concerning the sorts of benefits young people can get from a place like Hope Street. But the fact is that at the end of their time there, they are more confident and full of self-belief. Hope Street provides an environment in which young people can grow and experiment. Hope Street provides a form of training that promotes independence and not dependency. The value of independence was brought home to these young people especially vividly as part of an international exchange programme with similar youth organsations in Europe, during which young people from different cultures work together to prepare a public performance. As part of this piece of research a video of such an event was vieweed which clearly illustrated the physical energy and pleasure that young people got from working as part of team and doing things that they were good at. The self-esteem of the young people concerned was clearly bound up with their own body image and the fact that in a sense, their bodies had been liberated. Drama provided a means by which young people could find their inner potential. As one student commented,

> 'It broadens your conceptions. It widens your horizons about different cultures... It brings out what you already have inside. It brings you out of yourself. It brings you out of your shell.' (male, age 22)

As the above discussion suggests young people were, virtually without exception, extremely complimentary about the sort of training that Hope Street provides. The practical basis of the training was very popular, as was the fact that the Hope Street 'hierarchy' listened to what young people on their course had to say, and in this respect criticisms were few and far between. Some students felt that, if anything, the organization could be stricter to those students who failed to pull their weight. Others (not surprisingly) wanted more money or disliked written work, but all these were minor quibbles.

Regardless of the popularity of the training that Hope Street provides, the key question remains. What impact does this training have on young people's futures? How does 'Acting Up' and 'Workshop Leaders' affect both young people's perceptions of their futures and the reality of such futures? It is true to say that, at one level at least, many of those young people I interviewed had unrealistic ideas about where there passion for performance might take them. Many of those interviewed, and notably those who I interviewed in their early stages, talked about being famous whether this meant being a musician, a TV presenter or an actor. This was probably no more than bravado, but it is true to say that the practicalities of finding employment was not uppermost in their minds. The imbalance between the realities of arts employment and young people's ambitions creates something of a tension for the staff as one of the student's pointed out,

> 'they work you up. They all try and tell us that we're not gonna get jobs and your not gonna get that. But we all try and ignore them. We're like 'yeah, but we're all gorgeous and we're all gonna be dead famous.' (male, age 20)

Ultimately, the young people I interviewed did not expect to be famous, but it at least gave them a goal and a goal they did not have before. The young people I interviewed did not appear to be resigned to having to do jobs to survive, but were actually beginning to look forward to a future, where they can actually do work they enjoy. But there is still a genuine concern that the difficulties involved in getting a job is not paramount in young people's minds. For instance, I interviewed four people who were working on the 'Healthy Living' programme. All four of them said that they wanted to develop the workshop format after their time at Hope Street and set up an independent company designed to inform children about similar sorts of issues. This is a reasonable ambition, but the responsibilities, pressures, and difficulties in organizing such a project were the last thing on these young people's minds. They appeared to assume that such opportunities would somehow fall into their laps. This reflects a more general theme: that of avoiding independence. The young people I interviewed were undoubtedly more confident and more independent than they were before they arrived at Hope Street, but they were still reluctant to break off their links with Hope Street entirely. The year's support after the completion of training that Hope Street offers is an invaluable service and one that former students very much depend upon.

The 'Healthy Living' programme, at least provides a realistic bridge to the sorts of community based settings that many young people will eventually apply the skills they have gained. And on a very positive note, many young people talked about 'giving something back' to the local community. It is a great strength of what Hope Street does that this community-based rationale is not just a vehicle for training, but actively influences the sorts of work young people want to do.

The destinations of those young people who attend Hope Street are diverse. Some of those young people who had graduated from 'Acting Up' course commented that whereas some of their contemporaries had gone on to do arts-based work, many others had progressed onto additional courses at other local colleges in order to earn more formal qualifications such as a National Vocational Qualification (NVQ). The transitions which resulted from the implementation of the New Deal appear to have had a more predictable and indeed positive impact on young people's destinations. Of the seventeen young people who completed the first 'Workshop Leaders' course, four continued their work with Hope Street by joining up on the 'Transition to Work programme', six secured work either full or part-time arts-based work; two were working for a voluntary organization; two returned to full-time Higher Education; two were working for non-arts based organizations and the destination of the other remains unknown. The above represents an impressive measure of success, and reinforces the thoughts of the director I interviewed who hoped that in the future Hope Street can develop a more work-based culture in which paid projects such as the 'Healthy Living' programme become the norm.

There is no sense in which training courses such as 'Acting Up' and 'Workshop Leaders' can guarantee jobs. That is not their intention. Rather, Hope Street's achievement lies in the way in which it opens up people's minds to the possibility that they might have a future. The fact is that the responsibility to succeed ultimately depends on the individual's willingness to maximize these opportunities. As one interviewee put it, Hope Street dangles a carrot at the beginning of the course, and it's up to the individual to catch the carrot by its end. In other words, young people only get out of Hope Street what they put in. One of those interviewed who had completed her training put this very presciently,

'That's what Hope Street does. It gives you the vehicle to travel to the place you want to be if you wanna' be there. And if you don't really wanna' go that vehicle will break down.' (female, age 18)

Another young person described the Hope Street experience as 'explosive' in both an emotional and a physical sense. Most importantly, from an emotional point of view, the young people I interviewed felt like they belonged at Hope Street and that they were authors of their own training. They felt that the training they were undertaking had a purpose and that purpose was, ultimately, to help them find a job. Several respondents commented that Hope Street was over-powering in the sense that it was not just a training course, but in effect, a way of life,

> 'The course itself could become over-powering because you become emerged in it. It just becomes everything to you, it just means everything. It's just your destiny in life to complete it.' (female, age 18)

Perhaps this is why this form of arts-based training succeeds: because it belongs to the young people undertaking the training, rather those responsible for delivering that training. Perhaps Hope Street succeeds *because* its learning effects are secondary. The confidence-engendering nature of the course and the practical skills which can applied in a wide variety of work settings are not 'in yer face', but lie beneath the surface, and therefore have the additional benefit of giving young people a sense of control over what it is they learn. Above all, young people feel they belong at Hope Street. And they feel that the training belongs to them. As the director of the project pointed out the danger with discourses surrounding youth training is that such discourses amount to little more than talk. Youth training of this kind, however, has a concrete impact on young people's lives. The young people who attend Hope Street come from disadvantaged backgrounds in which being unemployed is the rule rather than the exception. Hope Street gives these young people belief. It opens them up to the possibility that they can be the author of their own careers as well as their own training. Herein lies its success.

The Portuguese case study

The labour market situation

Employment The Portuguese Youth Inquiry which was carried out in 1997 suggests that the period between 18 and 20 years of age is the most crucial in terms of who does and does not pursue their education. However, evidence suggests that at a national level, more than a quarter of young people start work before the age of 15 (TSER Report, 1999). The situation is such that even beyond the age of 20 young people, and especially young women, continue to be very **dependent** on their families for economic support. Young people are finding it very difficult to secure professional jobs, as, for instance, in the last ten years the number of qualified students has doubled. Since the beginning of the 1980s, however, youth unemployment has decreased, dropping from 69 per cent in 1980 to 45 per cent in 1997. Having said the overall proportion of those unemployed who are 'young' rose between 1992 and 1996 from 5 per cent to about 7 per cent. The age range of 15 to 19 years appears to most affected by recent economic change. In 1980 30 per cent of the unemployed came from this age group, by 1997 this had dropped to 11 per cent. This trend can largely be explained by the effort to expand education. It is also true to say that young people are delaying the search for their first job. 43 per cent of young people now look for their first job between the ages of 20 to 24 compared to only 30 per cent at the onset of the decade. This represents a marked change. In the 1980s about 45 per cent of first job seekers were aged 15 to 19 compared to 35 per cent in 1997. Of most concern is still the fact that those with less qualifications continue to feel the full brunt of unemployment. Nonetheless those who have better qualifications are more likely to be unemployed than they would have been ten years ago. In this context, the family plays a key role in supporting the most vulnerable young people. Such support is particularly important in a climate in which young people are liable to change jobs relatively often and to experience a period of unemployment. Unemployment has indeed become the norm for many young people (TSER Report, 1999). Young people from ethnic minorities are especially vulnerable in these circumstances. Even those young people who do secure jobs are likely to be subject to the insecurities of jobs with short-term contracts or indeed, no contracts at all (Almeida *et al.*, 1996).

The Portuguese transition system

Youth transitions in Portugal are very much determined by economic imperatives and by an ideology of enterprise (Azevedo, 1999, p. 83). Regardless of issues of quality, the Portuguese government is clearly determined to develop policies which provide young people with the skills necessary to support a thriving economy. And yet, young people's transitions remain unpredictable. In this climate the likelihood is that young people will continue to rely on a intermittent and insecure system that is characterized, above all, by the uncertainty of, as opposed to the predictability of, the future (Figueiredo, Silva and Ferreira, 1999, p. 118).

Education   The schooled population in Portugal continues to grow as a result of the prolongation of compulsory schooling and the more general trend towards a democratic educational service (Figueiredo, Silva and Ferreira, 1999, p. 98). At the secondary level, young people can pursue a general programme of study or a technological one. Both avenues can lead on to a University education. At this latter stage two possibilities exist: the attainment of the baccalaureate and graduate degrees; and a polytechnic education.

In recent years secondary and tertiary education has continued to expand at an unprecedented rate. Private and co-operative forms of education account for a significant proportion of this expansion. In 1993/94, one third of students in tertiary education pursued this route. More generally social change has encouraged a situation in which young women are increasingly likely to pursue their education and, ultimately, a professional career. But despite such positive developments an alarming percentage of young people are 'dropping out' of the system. Even those young people who to achieve qualifications are likely to struggle to secure the types of jobs to which they may aspire.

Training   In the Portuguese system professional training has its own special category: based either in the education system or in the actual labour market. Both forms of training are complemented by careers guidance services. The government strategy in fighting youth unemployment is to promote professional training amongst the most vulnerable of young people through the Professional Training and Employment Institute (IEFP) and to finance temporary programmes in which companies and organizations provide young people with temporary contracts of employment.

Statistical data is scarce in this area, but there are certainly strong indications that the above programme has had a limited effect (Dias, 1997, p. 443-449). Some commentators argue, in fact, that professional training is simply too specialized and as such has limited broad value beyond the benefits received by the companies (as opposed to the young people) it serves (Moniz and Kovács, 1997, p. 86). Such commentators call for a convergence of strategies between employers and training agencies which in turn co-operate with the government. Such a move would also require a radical change in the attitudes of entrepreneurs. At present training is simply not enough of a priority amongst employers for it to fulfil its potential. In particular, technological training is not popular amongst the young people who it targets. Indeed, it would be true to say that the young people concerned believe such training to have an inferior status to that of the professional training conducted within the general education system. Still according to Moniz and Kovács (1997): 'the continuation of the current situation leads to a imbalance of youngsters with University qualifications unable to find jobs, **while there is also** a lack of young people who have received professional training (Level III and IV)' (p. 83).

In accordance with the results of the last national inquiry into Portuguese youth:

> 'From the point of view of political and ideological rhetoric, vocational training is, nevertheless, assumed and divulged as a privileged device to promote professional knowledge that facilitates integration into working life, as well as professional valuation and modernisation, assuming itself as a vital resource to career progression. But the reality is that vocational training presents itself as a domain on the limit line of educational projects and professional trajectories of the majority of surveyed young people. And this because, they claim, that 'they never needed it' (3%), 'they are still studying' (28%), or simply because 'they never thought about it'.

> *I have never needed to attend any kind of vocational training*, is the main reason among two groups placed in diametrically opposed positions towards work: housewives (5%) and workers (49.4%). In these two categories, together with the unemployed, the reason *never thought about vocational training* also receives the highest score. This clearly indicates the discontinuity between political discourses and (re)qualification strategies set in motion or planned by some of the potential targets of those measures.' (p. 54)

One of the more effective policy changes was the creation of the Professional Schools, towards the end of the 1980s. As our case study is focused on a professional school course, it would be useful to discuss this particular aspect of the system.

Professional schools Created in 1989, professional schools constitute a sub-system of professional training. They provide initial professional training for young people between the ages of 15 and 18 years (Ministério da Educação, 1996). Professional schools are financed by the European Social Fund, as well as the state and the private sector. Such schools are however, relatively autonomous, pedagogically, administratively and financially. Their remit is to provide professional training and to promote the learning of transferable skills that can be applied in the workplace. The curriculum aims to develop young people both socially and personally and as such claim to be more than about simply 'training for the job'. The schools are, however, subject to a set of strict financial regulations. They are also characterized by a strong commitment to their local communities. Their main concern in this context appears to be the constraints of the bureaucratic process that envelopes them rather than the content of the training they provide. In this context, the political strategy underlying professional schools tends to be somewhat hazy. However the Director of Secondary Education describes professional schools as,

> '... a real alternative in the development of human resources that can give a global answer to the requirements of training of an increasing layer of youngsters that, for diverse reasons, can't find its expectations and needs in other training systems. But it is also an alternative capable of both integrating good practice and of encouraging the development of new innovative approaches.' (Ministério da Educação, 1996)

The Chapitô project

Chapitô (a name which emanates from the French 'Chapiteau' meaning circus tent) was originally the dream of the charismatic female clown, Teresa Ricou who became famous for her circus work in Portugal during the 1970s. The embryo of Chapitô, the *Mariano Franco* School was originally set up on a voluntary basis in the Bairro Alto quarter of Lisbon. But the school was moved to Costa do Castelo in 1990 when it was formalized with the introduction of the Course of Circus Expression. It was in 1991 that the current Professional School of Arts and Handwork of Entertainment (EPAOE) was established. Nowadays, Chapitô has various other roles and is currently the location for a Cultural Centre, a Library, and an Audiovisual Centre. It also runs evening classes and owns its own restaurant.

The pedagogical model For the delivery of the EPAOE training Chapitô operates according to a modular system, the aims of which are defined by the teachers of each discipline, in compliance with the general aims of each school year. The students on the course also play an active role in determining changes in educational provision. Chapitô aims to prepare its students for the working world and more specifically the world of entertainment. It therefore trains young people in various forms of artistic expression including music, dance, circus arts and theatre. The School prides itself in the contemporaneous nature of its curriculum which reflects the fact that the staff are all performers or producers outside the school setting. On the one hand the course has a clear professional function as a training ground for young performers, but on the other it encourages those same performers to continue their studies along similar lines. Students receive training in technique, performance and production.

The course of arts   In the above context two courses are provided: the Course for Arts and Circus Entertainment -'Arts' and the Course for the Handcrafts of Entertainment – 'Handcrafts'. The two courses function as two faces of the same coin, one of which works on-stage, the other on the back-stage. Both courses run for three years. In the course for Arts and Circus Entertainment several disciplines are integrated in three key areas: languages, science and technique. In a typical year the EPAOE would employ about thirty teachers, providing training for 80 to 90 students in 6 classes. Two third of students' time would be spent on the Arts component of the course.

The students   The project has always been targeted at young people who have problems fitting in with mainstream education. A typical student would have nine years of compulsory education behind them. Students come from all over Portugal and indeed, internationally, to attend the school, but are more likely to emanate from Lisbon and its peripheries. Many of these young people would have been unable to adapt their artistic bent to the constraints of school life. In contrast to the other two projects, however, most of them are in fact, middle class.

The respondents concerned began their training during the 1997/98 school year. Initially there were 23 students attending the Arts course. Most of them came from the Lisbon periphery: half from the south bank of the Tagus, the remainder from either Spain or the north bank of the river. They are all single and aged between 15 and 23. The girls are on average younger (19 is the mean age of the girls; the mean age of the boys is 21). The students arrived at the school with a variety of qualifications. Only one of this intake had formally graduated from secondary school. In terms of their parents backgrounds most of these young people come from families with a professional middle class tradition. The demanding nature of the course is reflected by the fact that 8 students dropped out of the course during its second year; this rate of attrition is partly explained by the fact that 5 Spanish students left to start up their own performance group. Nowadays, the number of pupils is restricted to a total of 15.

Some problems   The young people we interviewed did identify some problems with their experience of Chapitô. There was some concern that the school lacked equipment and materials which is itself a reflection of financial conditions that are largely beyond the control of the School itself. The uncertainty of funding is undoubtedly a problem for Chapitô. Many of those people with responsibility at the school simply do not have the necessary bureaucratic training. As the School Director commented during her interview 'Nobody that is a clown can manage such a big thing...' Establishing a balance between the demands of performance-based modules and theoretical and technical ones is also a concern. It is generally very difficult to motivate students in this particular area of the curriculum. As the School Director also pointed out many students 'are good in practical, but poor in theoretical subjects'.

In the above climate it is not always easy to maintain discipline. Many students lack respect for school rules. Some may have personal 'hygiene problems' and also find it difficult to establish 'equal' relationships with teachers. But perhaps the most pressing difficulty is the fact that the young people concerned become so passionate about their own projects that the wider demands of the curriculum tend to be neglected. There is indeed a worrying tendency for students to miss such classes. In their defence the students argue that there are simply not enough breaks between sessions, and that as a result their physical condition is such that they are forced to pick and choose classes. They also complain that there is a lack of technical subjects in their schedule. The teaching co-ordinator points out that a tight schedule is a result of the fact that the professionals deployed at the school work outside of its walls and therefore are only available at particular times. The organization of the school and in particular, of the school time-table, therefore constitutes a careful balancing act:

'Many things have to be taken into consideration: the structure of the modules, the relationship between modules, courses, and subjects areas and the year of study. A lot of projects are also going on in Chapitô. Meanwhile, the teachers are themselves a diverse group of people. There are also professional tests to be taken and qualifications to be achieved. All this in an environment in which people want to be creative.' (teaching co-ordinator)

Discussion

Through its development towards EPAOE Chapitô has emerged as a vocational school which prepares artists 'for the interpretation of artistic roles and to work as entertainers in socio-cultural projects' and/or to provide a superior degree of training in these areas. The School is based on principles of inter-disciplinarity between the several disciplines, is both practical and theoretical in nature, but is characterized, at lease to an extent, by its flexibility.

'...The course functions as a globalization of all the areas in only one school, only one day of work...' (male, age 20)

Creativity underlies everything the students learn, as does the onus on achieving individual aims in the context of the broader aims of the curriculum,

'In theoretical lessons for example we do not have books, as in the state school I attended. In this school the scheme of work is far more creative...' (male, age 20)

The young people interviewed were clearly under-motivated by theory-based lessons. However, such lessons are essential to a rounded education. The School is very much concerned with offering students a taste of everything,

'Normally they would separate the artistic phenomenon: or we have specialized theatre schools alone, or dance schools, or schools alone... but here they give us a little of everything. They give us a chance to try a little of each artistic area...' (group interview)

In this *'very cool place'*, most of these 'artists to be' found a school very different, compared with the more formal schools they were used to. Many students commented that they felt like they were *'living in family'* or in their *'second home'*.

'I don't like the other normal schools, the way of functioning, the relations with the school, the fact of people making things they don't like. In the other school I was doing something that I didn't like. It is very good coming for a school and be doing a thing that we like. Different ways, different people to be with people who like the same things...' (female, age 15)

'We are all equal and this is a family (laugh). Because this is a smaller school, all teachers know each other and know each of us. It's my second home (laugh). I spent more time here with teachers and friends than I do with my parents and my family.' (female, age 15)

Students are therefore more than aware of the distinctive character of the school which they attend. The fact that the curriculum actively engages with young people's interests is especially popular,

'I find this school is so open-minded. I can develop my own ideas. And in other schools I have things stipulated... It is a school open to new opinions and ideas.'(female, age 19)

The variety of the subjects students learn is also deemed a positive feature, largely due to the efforts in the part of teachers to articulate the relationship between different parts of the course.

'The disciplines are so divergent one from the others. But at the same time, have you ever seen the show at Cornucópia Theatre that I've seen. And the scenery had seven doors. And from each door appears a monologue or one sketch. They were unconnected but at the same time it all fitted together.' (female, age 19)

One student described the relationship with teachers as 'fantastic'. Students described their relationship with their teachers as a 'relationship between friends'. Teachers are indeed addressed by their first names.

'Here we are practically equal, they just know more than we do, that's the reason they are above us. The lessons aren't impersonal and you are encouraged to discuss any problems you have both in and out of the class.' (male, age 20)

This kind of relationship, however, is problematic, in the sense that many students are simply not used to this kind of a relationship with authority figures. They are not used to a school where opinions can be expressed so freely and where they as students have such an active role to play in the production and consumption of their own education.

Another positive benefit of the school is that it facilitates direct contact with art producers, creators and artists in general. This therefore provided a bridge to the profession and on occasions the opportunity to actually observe or even participate in professional productions.

'We went to Spain to see Cirque du Soleil. And since the moment I entered the tent it gave me goose bumps until I left. And when I had to leave I just didn't want it to come to an end. I wanted that it to last forever...' (female, age 19)

'[in Brazil] we were making a movie. It was a little bit strange, but it helped us understand the difficulties involved in making a movie, but the group of all the countries with whom I worked, was fantastic. I made some great friends. It was really good...' (male, age 20)

The feeling of belonging to this 'new family' helps to radically alter students' perspectives and indeed to raise their own expectations of life,

'In the beginning I had an aim: to be a juggler and an actress. Later, when I entered this fabulous school. Now I don't know what I want to do: I like everything.' (female, age 15)

Many students do not, however, see the course as an end in itself, but rather as a chance to assimilate the techniques and the tricks of the arts, and to use those abilities as a means of finding a new direction in life. The degree of freedom allowed in the school encourages young people to release their inhibitions and to find themselves. In particular, it encourages the mastery and the public expression of the body which is often altered physically through painting, hair styles, clothing and accessories.

'Now I'm very original. My mother says that I will become a stylist because I'm making these ridiculous clothing designs. (laugh)' (female, age 15)

The school encourages free and spontaneous expressions of individual performances, like singing, dancing and juggling:

'You can do everything you want to do. Your body moves itself even if you don't want to, you are always making something. And here I feel that I'm free. But I respect that freedom. Of course.' (female, age 19)

Young people appear to be searching for self-affirmation in the context of performance. They use the hedonistic images associated with performance as a means of finding themselves. In these circumstances their life choices are located between the individual ('to show the others what I can do) and the relational ('working as an entertainer'). This need to find a new direction in life was a common theme,

'What does this course teaches me? It teaches me everything. It teaches me how to relate with the outside world. I like to be with people who can teach me, so that one day I can also teach. And I find this school teaches me so many good things. It helps me to get to know my own body, it teaches me how to be, and it helps me to know myself a bit better and to know the others too.' (female, age 19)

This is a school where performers take their apprenticeship. They use their abilities and their bodies using and training their abilities to fulfil the demands on the performer. Their careers are tenuous. They are half way between the trapeze and the net; between flying and landing. One gets completed with the end of the other, in a succession of sketches reflecting a life of risk that is worth tasting, as long as the body permits, at which point the scene ends and the public either laughs or cries.

Motivations and expectations of youngsters in arts Chapitô offers the students the chance to pursue their dreams. It offers them hope that they can become what they want to become. The students themselves say they are motivated by two main factors, the opportunity to 'do whatever you want to do' and/or to assure 'a professional career in the world of arts'. Contaminated by the negative experiences they have already had in conventional schools the Arts appear to provide these young people with a 'cause for opposition' against the mainstream. Performance gives young people the opportunity to do what they want to do, rather than what the system says they should do. 4 out of every 5 of the students interviewed had some experience of amateur performance before joining the school. 70 per cent of the young men had partaken in circus activities; 46 per cent of young women had taken part in dance. But the main reason students gave for signing up for the course was a generic interest in learning the arts. Other reasons included the opportunity for self-improvement and the chance to learn theatre techniques,

> 'When I was a child, there was a place near home that had an activity called the Workshop of the Child, for children from 6 years (1st to 4th year). So I started to take part in theatre at 6 years of age. And I liked the experience and I wanted to carry on. I stopped because the group finished. Now I'm in a group, in Almada, that is the Cine-Theater of Almada and I wanted to go to a school in Cascais, but my stage manager spoke to me and said that here I would learn a little of everything, while in Cascais they only taught theatre. And I preferred to learn a little of everything.' (female, age 19)

> '[I came] because I wanted to have a career in the circus. My life has changed radically my way of seeing things. For example I was in another school and all I could think about was doing this. Since the first moment that I knew this was the school for me.' (male, age 17)

The young people interviewed came to know about Chapitô in a variety of ways, through their friends, family and perhaps the media. Some people's families were encouraging, others were dragged to Chapitô because it was 'their (parents') will',

'My mother passed here and saw 'Chapitô – Professional School of Arts and Handwork of Entertainment'. Then she decided to come in and ask what was it about. They had explained her and later at night my mother arrived home very happy: 'Look I discovered a school... you must like that school.' (female, age 15)

'I knew about Chapitô because one day I was passing there with lots of my friends at night and I saw a clown's shoes drawn on the door. Later on, one day I came here to see what it was and it was like I already knew the place. I came to this school against my parents will. The reason was my love for juggling. And because I wanted to stop doing what the others wanted and to start doing what I like to do.' (male, age 17)

Half those interviewed chose this arts-based course for professional training towards their intended careers in entertainment (mentioned mainly by boys) and theatre (preferred by girls).

Learning to be free These young people are, above all, young and their enthusiasm is boundless. In Chapitô they find the kind of sociability with teachers and colleagues and the sorts of freedoms that they were looking for but which they were never able to find in a 'normal' school. A common theme of the interviews was that being young was about learning how to be free, 'to know how to live' and to 'take advantage of all the moments in life', doing 'whatever you like'. They contrast this vision of being a young person with the idea of what is 'to be an adult': someone sitting back with a pair of slippers on who is constantly constrained by a routine full of obligations to do with children and taxes. These adults 'don't live'; the young people at this school self-consciously pursue adolescent lifestyles so they can do precisely that. These young people therefore define who they are against definitions of the conventional, the formal, and the regular. Knowing what they are not, by opposition to the adult world of order and conformity, they seem to find in the world of arts and entertainment, a fertile land for the affirmation of what they want to be, constructing an alternative identity within the context of youth sociability.

The identity they construct in this context is reinforced, for instance, by their musical choices that are actually about opposition and about not being commercial. They reflect the determination to be alternative.

'I don't like that commercial music, only for making people buy CDs.' (female, age 15)

As a group these young people are searching for what is different, for the eclectic and the unconventional,

> 'Nowadays there is no more that kind of sub-culture like the freaks and hippies... I think that is a bit a mixture of everything, because nowadays hippies are a mixture of freaks and dreads... and anarchists, of course. I am an anarchist.' (female, age 15)

On the other hand, we can equally find examples of young people determined to be unique.

> 'I am myself. I'm not worried about the image that I want to give and in belonging here. Or being here saying that this is a school of freaks and I have to become one of the freaks. No, I'm not having any of that. I like to be who I am.' (female, age 19)

Nonetheless the importance of being accepted as part of group and of asserting a professional identity is important to these young people,

> '[Now I'm] a normal person. I relate to all people. I don't have preferences. I listen, for example, to rock but to all types of music really. Even fado. I don't identify myself with anything. I'm a clown (laugh). My life is all about being a clown. (laugh)' (male, age 20)

These youngsters, come from area in and around Lisbon, and yet in general, seem to refuse to identify themselves with their local neighbourhood which they see as grey and characterless. The world of entertainment offers them something different and exciting.

Many of these young people have difficult relationships with their families precisely because they associate their families with the conventional and the predictable. These young people want to be provocative, they act and behave in ways that allows this, but this also provides a sound basis for their professional development. On the other hand, it creates a tension that the family is not always able to deal with. Compromise, is invariably a sensible solution to this problem,

> 'In the beginning they didn't agree very much, because [they thought] nothing useful was done here. My parents had come here to see [the exercise] and later they were convinced. My father, at least said that he liked it and he apologized, and later we cried. (laugh). At the end, he saw that all this was put together with real passion.' (male, age 17)

The alternative sources of identity which these young people have chosen therefore provide a foundation upon which they can begin to navigate their own futures.

Rehearsing their future pathways Two key aspects of young people's futures emerged during this research, their professional life and that of their families. The latter reflected the above concern that these young people are determined to construct unconventional lifestyles.

> 'I imagine myself as a person who is not going to have a normal life. At an emotional and a financial level.' (male, age 17)

Young people see their futures as inherently unstable. But this is not assumed to be a bad thing. They crave mobility and are determined to do 'everything'; to do what 'they like'', and their dream is to become part of those theatrical and 'new circus' shows that allow them to do just that. The new circus is that which focuses on a theatrical plot, interspersed with circus techniques, musical techniques and artistic forms of expression: those techniques are developed at the EPAOE courses and at the Chapitô Circus Company. The important thing is 'to be on stage'.

> 'My dream job now is to go work with a theatre group that is *Nós do Morro*. That is from the Vidigal slum quarter in Brazil. They were really fantastic people. they gave everything to me. I wasn't waiting for... They had given me friendship, love and an incredible affection and I will try to repay that because they have no way to access things that we have here at the circus. I want to try giving them that possibility to work with the circus. At the moment, that's **my dream**.' (male, age 20)

At Chapitô young people look to construct the foundations upon which they can construct their future dreams. Chapitô offers a name and a good reputation, because of the quality of the teaching, which is well known throughout the professional world of performance. To most of the Chapitô family members, the house is a place in which they can work towards their ultimate goal of artistic success.

The God's Trunk: a first year exercise The God's Trunk is an exercise which formed part of the assessment of the 1st year EPAOE pupils. This 'curricular exercise' took place in the end of the first module (in February of 1998) by the students of the two courses – 'Arts' and 'Handcrafts' – and involved the two groups working together in order to produce a show.

This play therefore provided an arena in which students could demonstrate the techniques they had learned including juggling, trapeze, expression, dance and rope. After little more than four months of lessons, the first year pupils were able to construct a play for public presentation to their teachers, family and friends and in doing so were able to demonstrate broader aspects of stage craft.

This performance allowed for artistic performance and the realization and pursuit of the following concerns: the relationship with the everyday; artistic impression; group dynamics; the production process; surprising or unexpected experiences and interpersonal relations. The approach the group adopted was about qualitatively critiquing social reality; to look at the 'real' world from a new perspective in order to unearth the meanings that lie underneath social practices and representations. The play constitutes the main object of this phenomenological approach, to be analysed and interpreted as a form of symbolic production.

The subjects picked for this exercise were freely chosen by the students. The class divided itself into working groups and each one chose a thematic area of the general subject: 'the Gods'. They conceived four main sketches dedicated to the subjects of the Gods of Earth, Air, Fire and Water (the four natural elements) all linked by three further gods: the God of Manipulation and its devils; the Goddess of Love; and finally, the God of Madness.

> 'The message [of the God's Trunk] was nothing. What it interested more at the moment was to show what I was learning in terms of techniques and the fact that we could choose what we wanted to do and how.' (Group interview)

The key theme emerging from this performance was the idea that television holds a dominant power over the world. The performance therefore constituted a form of social criticism of the global media. More important than the theme, however, were the working practices of the group,

> 'In these exercises they were always very anxious about 'what should we do? And if we can do everything, then what can we do?' And, the general rule, is that there is always somebody who throws the first stone.' (Pedagogical Co-ordinator)

Relations with everyday life   Having chosen their subject freely the real challenge was to operationalize the techniques they had learnt in that context. The group needed to be very organized, as the teacher co-ordinating the performance indicates,

'Whenever they present the exercise there is a meeting immediately afterwards to discuss what they have learnt and what they can learn from the experience. When I co-ordinated I tended to emphasize meeting schedules and fulfilling rehearsal commitments and such like. The onus of the meetings we had then were concerned with respect, being jointly responsible, the importance of being attentive to the others work and to self-evaluate, than on the level of the content. Therefore, the content, if has some relation to that level, is more about the level of technique: why such and such was such a funny idea for the model and it didn't work out during the editing process and this is a signal that you did not dedicate enough hours to do that and so on. So the aim was to identify and discuss problems. People can be fragile. But as everything comes from them, at the end this fragility is solved or surpassed and does not have a negative effect because of what you achieved. It was a pleasure to see what you achieved and now, about what you made we are going to see which are the most positive aspects and the most negative ones. Our intention is always, without devaluing the positive, to make them improve upon the negative.' (Pedagogical co-ordinator)

The performance did not call upon specific instances of young people's own life experiences, but such experiences nonetheless played a key role in the development of the performance.

A key concern here is what it is that actually distinguishes Chapitô's approach to performance and training? New circus undoubtedly plays a key role in combining a theatrical and circus-skills component to the overall performance. More importantly this approach is characterized by a form of social criticism, an approach that is self-consciously marginal and in opposition. This form of theatre has often been used historically as a form of social satire. These very same values may well have an important role to play in these young people's everyday lives. The Chapitô style is very distinctive in nature,

'a good example of secondary learning is the informal learning that goes on here in the esplanade or in the circus tent when they get together and learn from each other. That is the Chapitô style. When we compare photographs of the 1st year book and the same group of pupils in the 3rd year, some of them are unrecognisable. And all the exterior signals that resemble them piercing, painting or hair cutting, the hair badly cut, wearing the type of colour and the type of clothes, overlapping the clothes. Although I find that they don't actually take much of a step back and reflect about this. But it is a Chapitô style. Those signals represent a coming together of the group and of group consciousness. The school prioritizes individual needs but only within the group. It's people working together. This compels them to

respect others and to the notion that they are nothing without each other.'
(Pedagogical Co-ordinator)

The emergence of a group dynamic Because they were encouraged to take control of the process for themselves, the students became concerned about the way the process was organized and about the group dynamics that were involved in the process. The interpretative analysis that we made with the help of the protagonists disclosed relationships that developed according to perceived hierarchies, the assumption of leadership roles, and on the partnerships between those who had prepared the scenes. Some students worried therefore, that nobody was taking overall responsibility. Gender roles were another particular concern,

'Without wanting to fall into prejudice, it's true that Portuguese society is deeply conservative and very male chauvinist, the question of equal opportunities at Chapitô is a tricky one. Chapitô was founded by a woman, most of the teachers are women; women manage the place, but equal opportunities isn't in itself a pressing question. And, sincerely, never, but never, have I witnessed any situation that differentiated a girl from a boy, a woman from a man. Because as, as I said, the learning process is very much centered on the individual. If a man is a man then he is a man, and if a woman is a woman then she is a woman, but that just happens to be part of what they are, the countries they visit, or what they saw. It's not really a major concern. This artistic environment is a context where heterosexuality, homosexuality, everything here is very diluted. They perceive that this universe is not the archetype: woman is woman/man is man. Here exits a natural experience between people who are homosexuals, others that are heterosexuals and this is not about the marginalization of difference, but of people respecting individual difference. It's about mutual respect.'
(Pedagogical Co-ordinator interview)

Indeed, it is certainly true to say that Chapitô is a very liberal and accepting place. Gender relationships are not an explicit concern, they are played out in the school's everyday life, as are questions of race and sexuality. Questions of equality are therefore implicitly important to Chapitô. Chapitô is about accepting equality alongside plurality. Individual autonomy is the key.

The learning effects of the God's Trunk The God's Trunk provided the young people concerned with a whole raft of direct and indirect learning. As far as direct learning is concerned techniques were certainly improved, but so were aspects of responsibility at a personal and a group level. Indeed, the emergence of a sense of group solidarity and the boost in the mutual respect this entailed was the key indirect effect. At Chapitô formal and informal learning work hand in hand as a means towards the development of the professional circus performer. This particular exercise provided multiple forms of learning that have a personal impact as well as a professional one.

In the above context it is worth briefly reflecting on the less predictable elements of the Chapitô experience. At one level this was played out in the need to improvise both in terms of performance and the technical preparation for a performance. However, many of the unexpected aspects of performance reflected the informal nature of the training and the fact that some things were not as well rehearsed as they should have been. Having said that, this was a very important aspect of the training in its own right: the realization that groups and individuals are limited and how best to deal with such limitations.

> 'It turned me off being a director because people just didn't want to work. And it was hard for me as an equal to impose my will. How can I being in the same position tell them: 'You must work, you must do' when people do not want to do any of that stuff? If you're a teacher OK. they don't want to work and he says 'Work!'... There were many groups who started to work one week before, and that is totally stressful. It [The exercise] helps you to get to know people very quickly. It helped us develop relationships because we had to deal directly with each other. It helped us apply techniques. We knew that we just couldn't fail. In the lessons we can fail.' (Group interview with video discussion)

In this environment the teachers had very little direct input into the training process. The young people concerned, in contrast to examples of other more directive exercises were, in effect, given responsibility for their own training. Teachers only really dealt with resource problems. The young people concerned were therefore encouraged to take maximum responsibility for the project and, as such, were given more freedom to express their own creativity.

Conclusion

Young people are constantly looking to 'find themselves'. To them conventional schools and training projects are boring and oppressive. Meanwhile, the adult world is full of all sorts of responsibilities that they are determined to defy. Chapitô offers them a freedom and openness they simply have not experienced elsewhere. In this context Chapitô gives young people a wide variety of skills and experiences. Direct and indirect forms of learning are, in effect, the instruments used by young people to seek an effective transition into adulthood. It is especially important that young people are also subjected to very open relationships in which gender relations are more fluid and tolerant than they may be used to. More generally Chapitô encourages the development of an artistic identity and of a professionalism that is liberating rather than suffocating. In short, such a project actively promotes young people's lifestyles in contrast to the predictable norms of adult life. The Chapitô model therefore constitutes a holistic approach to training which uses performance as a means of integrating young people in a context in which they do not feel that they are being artificially forced to conform. Any individual weaknesses are thus confronted collectively. Young people are committed to this project because it is sensitive to their needs and to the needs of their peers. This project is prepared to invest time in unearthing young people's talents. This training is biographically reflexive. It focuses on young people's needs and gives them responsibility for their own development through symbolic production. Self-confidence is therefore the cornerstone of what is achieved at Chapitô. The experience of *The God's Trunk* production and of Chapitô in general is therefore based on providing a space in which young people are motivated to give part of themselves,

> 'I find that all the characters were in some way identified with the people. I find that each person was there to give a bit of themselves.' (Group interview with video discussion)

The decision to attend Chapitô is itself indicative of a young person's decision to choose to actively have a role in the trajectory of his or her own identity. Chapitô provides new horizons. It extends young peoples options in ways that they may not have thought possible. Many of those young people starting at Chapitô may not actually have the commitment and determination necessary for a professional career. However, their experience of Chapitô provides the foundations upon which they can begin to develop their own career ambitions. It gives young people the self-confidence to develop their own careers and their own projects often in contexts that can have an active impact on the local community and on local disadvantaged children and adolescents.

As we pointed out earlier, the young people attending Chapitô come from different backgrounds, the primary difference being between those who entered the course directly from school and those who did not. These two types of entrance certainly influenced the degree of individual students' personal development (cultural consumption and lifestyles) and the extent of their personal freedom, notably in relation to family relationships. In addition, some of those young people beginning life at Chapitô may have had some experience of performance, while others would not. The experience of Chapitô was such that any specific artistic interest were liable to be changed or at least added to. But what unifies all students at Chapitô were the freedoms and self-confidence they achieved by the end of their time at the school. Comments from one teacher sums up this point particularly nicely,

> 'If we think about the aerial performers as one set or if we think about the acrobats as another, both take on a real responsibility not only for themselves but for each other. Acrobatics start in the acrobatics with exercises that have to focus on concentration, self-respect and mutual respect. On hearing the others. That is the basis on which confidence develops.' (Teaching Co-ordinator)

Chapitô provides an experimental environment. Such experimentation is as much about self-discovery as it is about professional training. Perhaps this element of self-discovery is the key to a successful training programme. Perhaps, more importantly, it is the key more to a more successful future.

Chapter 5

'Catching the Trapeze in the Learning Society': The Evaluation of Case Studies

Having discussed each of the three training projects, in this chapter we want to bring the above findings together in an overall evaluation of the main findings of this research. Broadly speaking this evaluation can be divided into six complementary sections: the concept of learning as identity work, the connection between youth lifestyles, performing and learning with regard to young people's motivation, the means of art and drama for facilitating learning processes, the potentials and contradictions of informal learning, the effects of different structural contexts on informal learning and finally the biographic outcomes for the young people involved. It is important to say in advance that intercultural comparison in a stricter sense only applies to the last two sections. As the projects under investigation are not mainstream in none of the countries they stand for themselves rather than for a regional or national model. Perhaps the differences are even bigger between the projects and their respective national education systems rather than between them. However, due to the different conditions under which these projects work and the biographic outcomes for the young people involved differ and their comparison allows for a deeper insight into the prerequisites of learning opportunities for young people in their transitions to adulthood.

Learning as identity work

The first point we want to make is that all three projects start from a concept of learning that differs considerably from that applied most of the other programmes and measures young people are confronted with in their transitions to work. Rather than providing clear cut skills or professional qualifications in a more technical sense the process of *finding oneself* lies at the core. Expressions of participants like 'coming out of your shell' (Hope-Street), 'bringing out yourself' (JUST), 'feeling free and able to learn all' (Chapitô) indicate this very basic quality (and result!) of the learning proc-

esses taking place in the projects. It constitutes the abiding factor in determining the character of each curriculum and the learning experience in
general. This concept of learning comes near to what – especially in the
context of the discourse on lifelong learning and on 'soft skills' – has been
called 'learning to learn'; and it especially coincides whit what has been
introduced earlier as biographical learning or biographicity (see chapter 2).

So what do we mean when we talk about *'finding oneself'*? This notion
essentially refers to the development of *self-confidence* and *self-
consciousness* through learning experiences, which, in contrast to institutionalized settings such as schools and more conventional training schemes,
place much more emphasis on the person as a whole. In effect, such learning is embodied and takes into account the individual's specific interests,
experiences and above all, qualities. Performing arts and drama can be regarded as excellent arenas for this sort of a holistic approach to training and
the end result is a much more comprehensive learning experience. The
courses we evaluated provided a space in which young people felt they
could belong, a context, where 'ontological security' (Giddens, 1991) becomes an important precondition for the development of skills which self-
consciously promote individual autonomy in social contexts. In using the
notion of autonomy here, we refer to the ability on the part of the individual
to cope with the risks and uncertainties associated with modernity. Some
sense of autonomy, and the sense that you as an individual can cope, is absolutely essential to young people in a constantly changing world. Drama
and the performing arts promote an atmosphere in which such autonomy
becomes a real possibility.

The above is only possible insofar as the three projects constitute what
can be conceptualized as *'secure spaces'*. Young people need to feel that
they belong to a social context. The problem is that as far as conventional
training programmes are concerned this need tends to be ignored. The
'normal' learning setting is much far more likely to be based on competition and adaptation than on shared responsibility. Although it might be
argued that this socializes young people into the realities of the world of
work, unless young people are given autonomy they will be in no position
to engage effectively in that world in the first place. The projects are characterized by this deep interplay between independence and belonging: to
become independent is not solely related to personal skills, it is a competence which gradually develops within appropriately secure spaces. This
sense of security, at least potentially, results in positive learning outcomes.
However, it is important to remember that learning can only be facilitated,
there is no guarantee that it will always take place. The individual is ultimately responsible for his or her own learning outcomes. A key factor in

achieving such outcomes is nonetheless the provision of appropriate learning settings and spaces. All three projects provide spaces which young people colonize. In effect, that space is no longer space in which young people are trained. It becomes their space. They take ownership of that space and hence ownership of their own training.

Our interviews illustrated the fact that young people were gratified by the fact that the three projects give them the opportunity to meet people which they previously not had. . Above all, the projects provide an environment in which people are prepared to listen to them. They are, indeed, positively encouraged to present their own opinions which are genuinely valued. Their interests and personal sense of creativity, their sense of self, is no longer something they feel they should be ashamed of. Self-expression is positively encouraged in an atmosphere of mutual respect and acknowledgement. In a world of risky transitions, this sort of environment encourages communication and understanding between people of different backgrounds and generations. Above all, the three projects are not hierarchical in the traditional sense. The project leaders have authority, but their authority is negotiated and accepted rather than imposed which tends to be the case in more traditional types of training. The *inter-generational relationships* between students and teachers are founded on mutual respect, as opposed to a power differential.

A particularly significant way in which these projects have a positive impact is in the context of *gender*. The adults with which young people interact in these contexts are actively (although not necessarily intentionally or explicitly) engaged in introducing young people to alternative conceptions of what it may mean to be a man or a woman. The three projects provide an environment in which gender learning is able to flourish. The young people concerned may have been brought up with very traditional images of male and female roles and indeed, of sexuality. Due to their focus on learning in the sense of 'finding oneself' the projects provided an environment in which young people are encouraged to open up their minds in this respect. There ideas about gender are therefore challenged in such a way that they are able to develop their own understanding of these issues. These projects cannot guarantee that such gender learning has a long term impact on the young people concerned. However, they prepare the grounds for further experiences and developments in this direction. Gender learning is therefore facilitated in all three projects (including the all-male German case study which encourages participants to adopt different gender roles during the course of a performance). This is a good example of what we have called 'secondary' or 'indirect' learning effects. New practices of gender may not formally or explicitly appear on the agenda of any of the three projects, but such issues are dealt with in the day-to-day course of the projects. The fact that such issues are a 'natural' by-product of the training experience, rather than something that is fostered upon the young people concerned is probably a key factor in ensuring its success.

We do not want to imply that the three projects provide some form of an utopian arena for the construction of identities. Rather, they provide a secure foundation upon which young people can explore themselves. Young people begin to realize that there are possibilities they can explore and in doing so they are able to match their own skills with the new skills they are beginning to learn. This is a crucial component of identity construction. This kind of learning is not simply about learning a particular skill, but about using the learning of that skill to, in turn, learn more about yourself. It is therefore a much deeper, if rather less easily identifiable, kind of learning than that which is generally the product of training regimes. Our definition of identity is therefore not concerned with the achievement of stability. In contrast we see identity as 'acted out' in the three projects as a continuous practice which produces and re-shapes elements of biographic relevance. Wenger's (1998) especially pertinent work defines central properties of identity construction:

> 'Identity as *negotiated experience*. We define who we are by the ways we experience our selves through participation as well as by the ways we and others reify our selves.
>
> Identity as *community membership*. We define who we are by the familiar and the unfamiliar.
>
> Identity as *learning trajectory*. We define who we are by where we have been and where we are going.
>
> Identity as *nexus of membership*. We define who we are by the ways we reconcile our various forms of membership into one identity.
>
> Identity as *a relation between the local and the global*. We define who we are by negotiating local ways of belonging to broader constellations and of manifesting broader styles and discourses.' (Wenger, 1998, p. 149)

This process is not about individualization it is about locating the individual in a situation in which he or she belongs. It is about giving that person the opportunity to discover her- or himself in a supportive communal context. These projects provide a context in which young people can endow their own meanings in their own training. Intrinsic motivation for learning resides in the belief that that learning 'belongs' to the individual rather than to the trainer of the training programme itself. This is especially important for young people whose circumstances are such that any previous experience of training, as our case studies illustrate, is more than likely to have been an impersonal and negative one. In short,

> '...learning – whatever form it takes – changes who we are by changing our ability to participate, to belong, to negotiate meaning. And this ability is configured socially with respect to practices, communities, and economies of meaning where it shapes our identities.' (Wenger, 1998, p. 226)

The projects open up this learning circle through an emphasis on the fulfilment of a need to belong. Learning is not something that is achieved automatically. It can only be successful if it speaks to young people and if it gives meaning to their lives. Obviously performance and drama provide an appropriate framework for that.

Performing lifestyles: a key to learning motivation

Young people are encouraged to learn and they start to enjoy learning because they feel that this kind of learning is something they do for *themselves*. The key factor to initiate this motivation is the kind of meaning each of the three projects provides.

> 'All that we do and say may refer to what has been done and said in the past, and yet we produce again a new situation, an impression, an experience: we produce meanings that extend, redirect, dismiss, reinterpret, modify or confirm – in a word, negotiate anew – the histories of meaning of which they are part. In this sense, living is a constant process of *negotiation of meaning*.' (Wenger, 1998, p. 52)

'Meaning' is understood here in a very practical sense: participating in the projects is a source of 'meaning'; inasmuch it represents a space in which young people can begin to negotiate their place in the wider world. Due to the de-standardization and fragmentation of transitions youth this has become both increasingly important and difficult. As elaborated above (see chapter 2) this is the double function of young people's engagement in the development of lifestyles: 'fitting in and sticking out' (Miles *et al.*, 1998). On the one hand they have to cope with the structural demands of education and training, labour markets, family, peers etc., on the other they have to cope in a subjectively meaningful way, a way that allows a biographic narrative.

However, such meaning does not simply 'exist', rather it depends on specific situations and interactions, within which it is able to thrive. The projects we evaluated all provide a context within which young people could construct their own meanings. In general, training is formal in nature and is more concerned with the end product – a skill or a qualification – than the process. The potential young people have as active players enlivening this process is therefore neglected. The young people we interviewed made a totally different experience in both the courses we evaluated and the social settings in which those courses were run. This is because these courses transcend their basic function. In order to inspire young people they offer them more than a straightforward qualification. They offer young people a biographical alternative: a way of life. By taking part in a performance for example, young people take responsibility for their actions in a group context. Meaning is constructed through action and interaction. The young people concerned invest their own sense of self in developing the projects in which they are involved. The aim is to produce a successful performance and in order to achieve such an aim the individual becomes embedded in a setting of mutual responsibility and interdependence. As a result, the training and learning process is enriched beyond all recognition. This kind of meaning, based on communal activity, can therefore be identified as an important prerequisite for the achievement of deeper forms of learning. Motivation is not a question of personal ability, and should not be seen independently from the specific types of training in which they are involved. If young males and females are trusted to the extent that they are actively encouraged to experience expediency, agency, manageability, then motivation is unlikely to be a problem. In all three projects this interrelation can be observed.

The three courses can be described as 'communities of practice', which enable their members to engage in the negotiation of meaning, and which keep 'the tension between experience and competence alive' (Wenger, 1998, p. 252). In communities of practice, emphasis is as much on 'community' as it is on 'practice'. The community only exists through a 'common enterprise' – a project, a drama, a performance, and the practice becomes endowed with meaning because it is part of this common enterprise. In this context, the three projects can be described as what Skelton and Valentine (1998) call 'cool places' (Skelton and Valentine 1998); they provide meeting points with which young people can readily identify. In this respect, e.g. Chapitô provide a social space which offers a specific lifestyle which young people actively want to be identified with. Styles are markers of a group, they can be, as in the case of Chapitô, markers of a common identity,

> 'Style, as it is manifested through dress, look, sound, performance, and so on, is a powerful means of giving a group validation and coherence. It functions perhaps rather like the 'totem' according to Emile Durkheim (1915), as something which gives visible expression to an individual's sense of belonging to a group – of belonging to something which compensated for the lack which characterizes 'individuality'. It allows a group to recognize itself and to be recognized (although not necessarily 'understood') by others; it makes a 'statement' which can be sent across the group as well as directed beyond. Indeed, subcultural style is always relational in this sense, measuring itself not only against internal distinctions but also against much wider contexts.' (Gelder, 1997, p. 373)

Styles provide an important means of communal identification. At Chapitô, the youngsters use hair-cuts, clothes, body-piercings and tattoos in order to identify themselves as 'belonging' to Chapitô.

In considering the above arguments it is clearly the case that the three projects provide avenues of experience that are not usually available to young people. They provide them with a new perspective on significant aspects of their lives.

Arts and drama as vehicles of learning

In the above context it is clearly important to ask why it is that these projects appear to be so successful. One of the key findings of this research is that performing arts are a particularly fertile arena in which young people can begin to 'find' themselves. But why is it that artistic expression is so effective in this regard?

The three projects under discussion are in some ways very similar and in others very different. In terms of similarities, an artistic education allows young people to acquire technical training in order that they can go on to performance in public, whether that performance be in a theatre or as part of a circus. We can therefore identify a number of direct learning effects such as drama expression, dancing technique, acrobatics, juggling and musicianship. Above and beyond these direct learning effects all three projects offer young people a series of informal learning effects. Such effects have a fundamental role to play in such young people's personal and social development, and can include an increase in self-esteem, trust in oneself and in the others, boosted motivation, a sense of personal and professional accomplishment, security, and knowing how to work.

Drama and other performing arts actively facilitate the acquisition of these informal skills in a variety of ways. Drama, in particular, puts young people in a situation in which they develop their own sense of creativity and the confidence that emanates from that creativity. Performance also provides young people with a means of self-expression, a 'safe space' in which they can perform with confidence and in which they are accepted as individuals. Public performance also encourages such students to believe that they have something worthwhile to offer. The fact that their work is deemed to be worth watching boosts young people's belief in themselves. The process involved in performance and the way in which that performance grows is a great source of confidence. As one German participant put it: 'We are getting better in our performing. It is great to observe this'. This combination of explicit and implicit curricula gives young people a more rounded education and a broader spectrum of skills and competencies. Such training can thus be described as an 'integrated' learning model which promotes individual autonomy.

The choice of performing arts for achieving such learning processes as well as the particular practices and methods applied in all the three cases more or less directly derive from the work of the Brazilian playwright and theatre director Augusto Boal. In his concept 'Theatre of the Oppressed' (1980) he introduces theatre work as a viable means of empowerment:

> 'Latin America is a continent soaked with blood. There the Theatre of the Oppressed has emerged. Here in Europe such atrocities do not exist, not any more. However, this does not mean that in Europe there are neither oppressed nor oppressors. And if there is oppression there is the need of a Theatre of the Oppressed – that is: a Theatre of Liberation. The oppressed ... have to discover their ways to freedom, they have to rehearse the actions that lead them towards freedom. ... The Theatre of the Oppressed does not provide recipes for liberation, no ready-made solutions. Theatre of the Oppressed means dealing with a concrete situation, it means rehearsal, analysis, search.' (Boal, 1982: p. 68)

The first motive for Boal was to make theatre with people and not for people, to overcome the separation between active actors and passive audience. A characteristic of all forms of Boal's theatre – which are 'newspaper theatre', 'invisible theatre', 'statue theatre' and 'forum theatre' – is that they do not start from a given drama piece.

'The Theatre of the Oppressed starts from two premises: The actor, a passive being, shall become the protagonist of action. The theatre not only shall deal with the past but also with the future ... The spectator who has been capable for an act of liberation in a forum theatre performance will wish to pursue this act also in real life, not only in the fictive reality of theatre. The 'rehearsal' prepares him for real life.' (Boal, 1982: pp. 68, 69)

It is the group of players to decide on an issue of common interest, to discuss this issue and to develop the play and the performance. Thus, the process of activation starts already before the performance. All three projects under investigation share this approach at least insofar as all the plays or performances are developed by the young people involved. The transition from rehearsal to performance to lived freedom is a learning process for which the reflection and research of the players on the issue of interest is the starting point. As a consequence the courses start with preparing the players for this process. First they have to (re)search what they want to express, then they can start to experiment with forms and techniques of expression.

The two main dimensions on which this preparation happens are the self and the group and in all three projects they structure the first part of the course. On the one hand, practices of body experience are central for first feeling, then finding oneself – the body being the means of perception and expression of reality at the same time. On the other hand, the beginning of the course is about group formation. By both group discussion and collective physical practice a climate of trust and community, of mutual empowerment is developed. In addition to that in Hope Street explicit rules have been set up for constructive criticism during group sessions. These initial community building is then channelled into a common enterprise – the developing and realizing of a play, a show, a performance. In this process individual strengths and weaknesses are embedded in and complemented by the joint efforts of all and only thus become visible to the public.

Interestingly, many young people referred to the group when responding to the question what they saw as most effective in building up their self-confidence. Some young people from Hope Street reported from a first deception when realizing that it was not a 'real' theatre course which however revealed to be much more and much better after a while. One could assume that it is rather the group processes than the performing arts that account for learning and empowerment. But at least, performing arts are effective in attracting and motivating young people to social education and to allow for intense processes of group formation.

In this respect Wenger's discussion of 'communities of practice' is enlightening. Hisapproach defines learning as a principally interactive process. Individuals negotiate objectives and the meanings endowed in those objectives. Whereby they reproduce and develop their group relationship and achieve shared goals by joint action. Learning constitutes the 'fine tuning' which is necessary in this process: with regard to the individuals' subjective interests and those of the other group members, with regard to the complementing of strengths and weaknesses of the individuals involved, between the joint resources and abilities of the group and the requirements of the goal to achieve, and – last not least – with regard to the structural conditions in which the community is embedded (Wenger 1998).

Taking these properties of performing arts and drama into account they prove as an excellent context for designing for informal learning processes.

Informal learning: potentials and contradictions

It should not be forgotten that direct forms of learning clearly play an important role in the success of these projects. It certainly should not be assumed that the more informal a project the more likely it is to succeed. Such a proposition would be entirely misleading. However, there is a case for suggesting that informal learning has a very significant impact on young people and on the chances of pursuing a career. That career may not even be directly to do with performance, but it is very likely to require the sorts of skills young people acquire through informal learning. We are therefore obliged to ask the question: what is informal learning (cf. Coffield 1999)?

It would not be an exaggeration to suggest that most of the learning we undertake during the life-course is informal in nature. However, Holzkamp (1993) points out that learning is a central component of everyday life and plays a key role in relating the individual to his or her wider social context. Learning can be either expansive insofar as it allows the individual to extend the degree of his or her own agency or defensive, that is, it propagates against the loss of agency. It can be further argued that expansive learning is far more likely to generate intrinsic motivation whilst defensive learning is related to extrinsic motivation. The sort of learning we are describing here can therefore be seen to be expansive and the motivation as intrinsic as closely related to individuals' identities.

Thiersch (1986) agrees that learning can be very pragmatic in nature. An individual develops strategies to deal with the problems and dilemmas of everyday life. Everyday life is inherently limited by its routine nature with all the gendered and age-specific notions implied by that routine. As a result the learning process is completed when the problem is solved. The degree to which this type of learning is possible also depends on the impact of social inequality and uneven relationships which serve to constrain agency. In this context, it might be suggested that the informal learning offered by these projects provides a means of offsetting these inequalities.

Meanwhile Kahane (1997) argues that the post-modern condition of uncertainty, chaos and complexity is increasingly favourable to codes of informality. Where formal institutions fail in reproducing social order individuals are thrown back to active informal arrangements. He distinguishes a range of properties related to the informal code which can also be observed in the analysed projects as relevant factors of learning (see Kahane 1997, pp. 26-30):

- *Voluntarism*: a relatively constraint-free pattern of choice leading to a deep commitment.
- *Multiplexity*: a wide spectrum of (equivalent) activities enables individuals with different strengths and weaknesses to participate.
- *Dualism*: simultaneousness of different orientations offers the possibility to experiment with contradictory patterns of behaviour.
- *Symmetry*: balanced reciprocal relationships facilitate the acceptance of universal values.
- *Moratorium*: a temporary delay of duties and decisions allows for trial and error.
- *Modularity*: the eclectic construction of activities facilitates to take advantage of situational opportunities.
- *Expressive Instrumentalism / Pragmatic Symbolism*: combination of activities performed for their own sake and as a means for future goals respectively the symbolic surplus of goal oriented action increase attractiveness and allow for identification.

The lesson to be learned from this evaluation is that informal learning has considerable potential regardless of the pedagogical model being deployed. Very often this takes the form of a 'hidden curriculum' which supports the formal curriculum. All three projects illustrate the benefits of a multi-faceted teaching strategy which incorporates different kinds of teachers, different types of learning settings and learning contents which in combination can actually make 'the difference'.

There are two key dimensions to the informal learning provided by these projects. The one is the emotional quality of interpersonal relations and the second the existence of individualized and participative curricula which relate to young people and provide them with dynamic learning contexts. Even in the most formalized of the cases, Chapitô, the *relationship between teachers and students* is highly informal, and such represents a considerable contrast to the somewhat distant relationships that tend to develop in more formal settings. But it is precisely for this reason that many of our respondents described Chapitô as a 'family' or a 'second home'. The emotional quality of the teacher/student relationship is an important factor in determining the success of the learning experience. If young people have some form of investment in their relationship with their teacher, they are more likely to invest more of themselves in their training. As regards *individualized* and *participative* curricula, each of the projects recognizes the specific characteristics of their students and provides a curriculum suited to their needs and interests. This contrasts with mainstream schools which almost inevitably produce curricula aimed at a mass audience. The curricula we have studied are also participative in that they emphasize the importance of interaction. The relationship between the individuals' needs and their social relationships is therefore fundamental to any young person's experience of these projects (cf. Field 1999). The social embeddedness of (informal) learning however does not only regard the relationship between teachers and students but also among students or course participants themselves. Considering the immense role of the group in all three projects it can be said that they facilitate *peer learning* as young people learn from each other. Mørch argues that individual biographies increasingly evolve under conditions of fragmented contextualization (Mørch, 1999). Learning processes therefore depend on social interactions with other individuals who share common experiences and orientations. Inter-generational relationships in which the young learn from the adults are only one possible learning arrangement which is not valid for all learning contexts. More and more contexts therefore are structured by peer learning – the most famous example being the world of information and communication technologies.

These three projects provide settings in which young people develop personal, relational and technical tools for facilitating transitions into adulthood. It has been shown that performing arts in particular allow for processes of informal learning. The appraisal of such informal learning is central for these projects. However, this includes also structural limitations and contradictions: informal learning is not measurable. Thus it is difficult to assess and therefore it is not recognized by society – neither by the formal education system nor by employers nor by agencies as vocational counselling or employment service. For the young people this means that their possibilities to transform these learning experiences into further career options are limited. For the analysed projects this means difficulties in attracting public funding and legitimation but also in assessing the effectiveness of their work internally. They find themselves in a dilemma between accepting their peripherical status for the sake of the informal learning approach or they compromise with the formal education system which means to become subject to standardization in curricula and evaluation. As a consequence of formalized success criteria the access thresholds rise and the courses get selective. The dilemma is either to accept limitations with regard to the organizational stability and the recognised value of the outcomes or to partly renounce to helping those with the most restricted opportunities. This dilemma would only be resolved by assessing individuals' informally acquired skills, knowledge or competencies. However, the methods for the evaluation of informal learning largely depend on face-to-face-communication and are therefore situation- and context-related. They require time and they are in contradiction with the meritocratic function of qualifications and/or more labour-market related skills. Thus, they are unlikely to be implemented to a considerable extent. (CEDEFOP 1997; 1999).

In the following sections we will relate the three projects to their structural contexts. This will enable us to compare differences in utilizing the potentials of informal learning and performing arts in different context as well as their biographic effects on young people's.

Structural contexts of informal learning

After all that has been said about informal learning it would be misleading to suggest that each of the three projects is characterized by the same degree of informality. The three courses provide a vivid illustration of the value of informal learning, but the degree of such informality varies.

Table 5.1 Dimensions of formality in JUST, Hope Street and Chapitô

Dimensions of formalization	JUST	Hope Street	Chapitô
Relationship teachers/students	**Low**	**Low**	**Low**
Curricular	Low	Medium	High
Organizational	Low	Medium	High

JUST is a community-based project aimed at Italian and Turkish immigrants which is entirely voluntary and informal in nature. The courses offered by Hope Street, meanwhile, are somewhat less informal especially through the impact of the New Deal. The pedagogical philosophy underlying Hope Street is informal, but it nonetheless has to operate within more formal parameters than JUST. Chapitô is the most formal of the three projects. Despite its informal character, it is well and truly embedded in the formality of the Portuguese education system. The three case studies can be placed in a scale of learning formalization, which table 5.1 intends to demonstrate.

At this stage it is important to consider the broader contexts in which the three projects operate and, in particular, their relationship with the local community. The three projects are remarkable in the extent to which professional performers were able to apply their skills to fulfil a genuine social need. They were able to do something about changing the lives of: young people in Lisbon living on the street, something that was a central concern in the early days of Chapitô, or those who withdraw from the school system; the migrant, unemployed young people at risk of drug addiction in the case of JUST in Mannheim; and the young people for whom Hope Street provided a way out from the dead ends of the labour market at Liverpool.

None of the three projects is set up to provide comprehensive training for entrance into a particular profession. Rather they aim to provide young people with the confidence to face the challenges of the future. Their achievement lies in motivating what used to be very de-motivated young people through 'communities of practices' in which they are confident enough to establish who it is they are. They provide a reference point, a source of support for young people who, almost without exception, are deeply embedded in their local communities. The relationship between the projects and their localities is therefore crucial in providing the sort of support they need to pursue their present and their future. Young people, jobs and local communities come hand in hand. But each project has a different relationship with its local community. JUST represents the most local in scale and operates on a neighbourhood basis; Acting Up/Hope Street serves the city of Liverpool, whilst also organizing international exchange projects. The substitution of the Acting Up project by the 'Workshop Leaders' programme clearly states the investment Hope Street has in its local community. It is very important to maintain local links, because it is in the locality that young people will secure jobs and careers. It is very unlikely that many of these young people will become stars of the screen and the stage. They are more likely to secure jobs in local community projects. And Chapitô has a close relationship with the city of Lisbon and its surrounding area while simultaneously operating a variety of national and trans-national networks. Chapitô Circus Company often tours abroad while its students often receive offers of work overseas. Although social intervention may not be as much a priority for Chapitô as it was, links with the local artistic community have been strengthened and in doing so it has gone out of its way to match the cultural needs of the local community with those of the school. Regardless of the scale of the projects each operate according to a three-way relationship between the students, the projects and the community. Table 5.2 provides an overview of how the three projects have developed differently in the course of their history.

Each one of the three projects commands national and/or European public funding. However, the irregularity and uncertainty of funding constitutes a constant headache as the organizations concerned are always having to answer to public bodies despite the fact they are, nominally at least, independent organizations. CHAPITÔ is a professional school and provides vocational training, but also provides the home for a voluntary association. Acting Up was a pre-vocational course set up by the training organization, Hope Street, as a partnership between Liverpool City Council and the Everyman Theatre. The acknowledgement by the Merseyside Open College Federation and the selection as a New Deal provider have lead to more formal structures in terms of organization, curricula, principles of access and outcomes. In contrast, JUST is a (mere) community youth work project and it is run by a community centre depending on the city council.

In the above circumstances some degree of formalization is essential to the future of these projects. Certainly in the case of Chapitô and Hope Street such institutional links made regular funding a much needed reality. On the one side, as far the organizers of these projects are concerned, this has also resulted in stricter rules of management and evaluation which will inevitably wear down some of the informal aspects of the projects. Such developments have increased the vocational focus of these two projects at least. On the other side the profile of target groups has changed in both projects. A key question therefore remains: how far are professional imperatives compatible with an underlying ideology of informality?

Table 5.2   Starting positions, challenges and current positions of the three study cases

Case Study	Starting Positions	Challenges	Current Positions and Aims
ACTING UP/ HOPE STREET (Liverpool)	1989 Hope Street was set up (partnership between Liverpool City Council and a theatre) to run training programmes for unemployed youngsters	Originally bound up by priorities of the theatre 'Hope Street' got independent (1993); 'Acting Up' emerged as a pre-vocational course for young unemployed in social education, music and drama (accredited by The Merseyside Open College Federation) The 'New Deal' programme (1998) invested in Hope Street – replacement of Acting Up by the Workshop Leaders Programme	'Workshop Leaders' programme complemented by the 'Transition to Work' programme within which one group develops an educational programme to inform children about sex education or 'Healthy Living' in a way that relates to their everyday lives. Aims: Consolidating the more applied and vocational approach which is lead even more by the needs of the community (where young people are most likely to get the jobs)
CHAPITÔ / EPAOE (Lisbon)	Creation of Circus School Mariano Franco Animation work with minor people under tutelage of Justice Set up of the voluntary association 'Colectividade Cultural e Recreativa de Santa Catarina', with a wider artistic role	1987/88 Creation of Circus Course 1991 Creation of CHAPITÔ (Professional School of Arts and Handwork of Entertainment)	Chapitô's universe: • CHAPITÔ • Cultural Association • Circus Company • Library • Audiovisual Centre • Evening Courses • Restaurant • Intervention near minors under tutelage of Justice Aims (CHAPITÔ): Qualify young students to develop an artistic or performance career or go on to pursue further studies

| JUST (Mannheim) | 1980s: Development as youth club of a community centre in an inner city neighbourhood to offer leisure time activities (like music and drama) and to provide support for young people on a wide variety of issues their concern. | 1995: Three year funding to establish a youth drop-in centre (by the Ministry for Family, the Elderly, Women and Youth)

JUST was set up as a community youth work (a drama group initiated by an actress and drama teacher of Italian origin) | Selected as a pilot project for 'vocational preparation in the neighbourhood' by the Ministry of Labour

Aims: Promote development of personal and social skills and competencies to develop, with confidence, individual projects of socio-professional development |

The extent to which a formalization of such informal settings is possible in a given context as well as the effects of such formalization depends on the institutional context of the projects. Especially the structure of the national education systems need to be considered as they define both the recognized skills, knowledge and competencies and the institutional limits of education:

- The development of *Chapitô* coincided with a fundamental reform of the Portuguese education system. In order to increase the participation rate in education and training (being still the lowest in the EU) pathways that both were likely to motivate potential drop outs and met the demands of a modernizing economy were included in the formal system of vocational education. After nine years of compulsory education the professional schools' three year courses provide a more practice-related alternative to the academic pathways, yet keeping the young people in the education system. The process of formalization thus was rather fast and encompassing as regards the external aspects of funding, curricula and qualifications. At the same time the organization managed to keep the internal structures rather formal. However, it has to be noted that compared to the initial phase when addressing mainly street children the target group has shifted to a milieu of alternative middle class kids who are fed up with normal school.
- Also the development of *Hope Street* only can be evaluated with regard to larger trends in the UK in the nineties. On the one hand the education system has be flexibilized in terms of broader access and options to shift between different routes. Qualifications have become modularised in a way that single elements of education and training can be accredited and combined in an individual education portfolio; and – what is as

important – most options are combined with education or training allowances. This made it easier for organizations like Hope Street to become acknowledged without having to change totally. On the other hand, especially in the de-industrialized cities of the North, cultural industries and the community initiatives of the Third Sector have experienced a heavy promotion in order to develop new employment opportunities. Thus, it was possible to keep the focus on performing arts in a (yet reinforced) community perspective. However, in contrast to the times of the (rather pre-vocational) Acting Up project the recruitment for the Workshop Leaders programme considers the abilities of applicants to cope with the higher level of training and to achieve the qualification.

- The case of JUST can not that easily be described as a linear development. As part of a youth and community centre it largely depends on local youth policies and integration measures for migrants. Being strictly separated from the education system in institutional terms youth work in Germany is not recognized as a formal part of the transition system; and there are no signs that this will change in near future. This accounts also for employers who still trust more in formal qualifications than in more informal recruitment strategies. In the project's struggle for additional funding this fragile position becomes visible. When being part of a national programme for drug prevention in the mid of the nineties the open and informal approach was recognized for its efficiency in reaching the target group. In the end of the nineties the project was included into a local network for employment funded by the National Ministry of Labour. For this funding stronger formalization and standardization were required however without rewarding this by accrediting the elements of informal learning. Due to the limited perspectives of formalization no changes regarding the target group and the concept are necessary. The project can 'afford' to address the group of the most marginalized and to apply the Theatre of the Oppressed without having to adapt it to formal curricula structures.

This comparison shows that the potentials and limitations of informal learning strongly depend on the structural context: not only the national education system but also the local labour markets. On the one hand we find systems that are less institutionalized or institutionalized in a more flexible way. Here, informal learning projects have a higher probability to achieve funding and recognition. However, this makes them also more vulnerable for being included in a more bureaucratic organization of learning. A side-effect of this formalization is the rise of the entrance threshold privileging those who are more likely to cope with a vocational education curriculum. On the other hand we find a context that is rigidly structured by standardized vocational training. Here, informal learning is highly unlikely to become recognized by both the education system and the local labour market. If included into (and funded as) transition related policies this is viewed as an emergency social policy rather than as a reform of education policies.

After having compared the different structural contexts of the three projects we are able now to assess the biographic effects of informal learning in the performing arts for young people in their transitions from school to work.

Biographic effects of informal learning and performing arts

In some ways the three projects we have evaluated are very different in nature. They represent a response to very diverse transitional systems and the strategies they have adopted reflect this. However, there are common threads that unite these projects. Each of them seek to empower socially excluded young people. They provide these young people with a new source of learning and fulfilment. Performance emerges as a source for a wide variety of life skills, but perhaps more significantly as an arena within which young people can find themselves and can feel they belong to a social context which means something to them. Each of the three projects offer informal learning as a springboard from which young people can develop as individuals and as individuals with career aspirations. In effect, young people are empowered by the fact that they belong in their local communities; they are accepted as human beings and they can pursue their careers with renewed confidence and ambition. The virtue of these projects lies in the confidence they invest in young people as the authors of their own futures. In turn, these projects hint at a future in which educational models have the needs, motivations and creativity of young people at their very core.

To sum up, the courses provide a framework in which young people can begin to pursue the above. The ability to do so is the by-product of secondary or informal learning:

• The projects provide space for negotiated experience, precisely because they follow participatory curricula, where young people's interests and concerns are prioritized.

- They promote community membership, insofar as they establish a group experience which becomes increasingly influential in the way in which it fulfils young people's need to belong.
- They provide a particular learning trajectory, which encourages young people to believe that they have some control over the direction in which their lives will go. This increasing self-responsibility for their own lives is motivated by very concrete learning experiences.
- They represent one important context in young people's everyday experience which they learn to reconcile with, and indeed use to positively inform, other aspects of their lives.
- They encourage a relationship between the local and the global, insofar as they link personal concerns to broader social, political, cultural and economical ones such as migration and social exclusion. The young people concerned may not describe themselves as political, but the projects encourage them to deal with these sorts of issues through performance and in relation to their own experience of them.

It is worth reiterating the fact that the effectiveness of informal learning is dependent on young people investing such learning with the necessary commitment and motivation. But informal learning does not work entirely alone. Its success is dependant upon it working alongside more formal aspects. The student benefits from the fact that the projects do not formalize certain aspects of their training. They are therefore able to claim ownership of these aspects themselves. These projects therefore provide young people as one young person at hope Street described it, as 'a way out'; a way out from exclusion on the basis of social background, ethnicity and gender. These learning 'cocoons' provide an ontological security alongside a sense of belonging, often in environments whose only real sense of belonging was formerly based in a tradition of unemployment. The rhetorical notion most applicable to this discussion might well be said, therefore to be that of *empowerment*. The over-use of this term has tended to make it a hollow one, to the extent that it is apparently used to legitimize any form of public socialization or education. However, the origins of empowerment as a philosophy (e.g. Rappaport, 1981) are far more critical in nature. It is in this critical context that this term is appropriate here, insofar as there is a recognition that many young people do not have the resources to take up many of the opportunities that are available to them in theory. The three projects under discussion succeed in channelling individuals towards the resources they need in order to take advantage of such opportunities. They do so by respecting the individual regardless of how 'normal' or 'deviant' he or she may be. They also seek to raise young people's awareness of the opportunities available to them; encouraging them that they do have a future. They also focus on young people's strengths (which are often unutilized or even ignored) rather than their weaknesses. Finally, they provide supportive social networks.

The difference between conventional transition policies and the empowerment approach may be illustrated with regard to the social categories of gender and ethnicity. Many conventional training programmes do not acknowledge the fact that there is a strong tendency for young women to be orientated towards typically 'female' occupations as a means of propping up the service economy. Indeed, in truth many schemes for young (or reentering) women do no more than provide low qualifications in exactly these fields (e.g. home economics), thus ensuring young women's disproportionately low status. A similar pattern exists for young people from ethnic backgrounds. Instead of their bi- and intercultural and language competencies (which may well be applied in the realms of international trade or tourism for example) being assessed for their own sake, they are in actual fact generally compared to the formal standards and qualifications of the majority culture against which they compare, on the whole, unfavourably.

In the above two examples there is clearly a power deficiency. An effective programme of training needs to address both social and psychological dimensions of power. It needs to provide the social conditions in which empowerment becomes a realistic possibility, whilst ensuring the individual is allowed to grow as an individual within those conditions. All three projects prioritize this latter aspect of empowerment. This reflects the fact that any intent to provide the appropriate social conditions is rendered obsolete without an explicit recognition that individuals cannot be blamed for the fact they are excluded from other forms of education, training or work. The relationship between the organization and the individual is therefore an important one that has to be nurtured in order that the young people concerned feel that they can claim ownership for their own training biographies.

What we are describing here is a deep form of learning which in many ways is more ambitious than so-called 'primary' forms of learning. It is a form of learning based on the construction of identity rather than the learning of measurable skills. This form of learning may well encourage and provide young people with the confidence with which they can pursue more flexible careers. However, we do not mean this form of learning can singlehandedly solve the problems inherent in young people's transitions.

The projects under discussion deal with the symptoms of risky transitions. They help young people learn to find their own way in life and they motivate them to actively search for this own way. But the risks inherent in the transition to adulthood will nonetheless remain. In this regard we can take up the comparative perspective of the last section with regard to the effects of participating in such projects on young people's biographies. We have shown that the three projects differ in the form and the extent in which they are recognized by and linked to the formal transition system. Whilst all young people have described the learning effects with regard to their personal and social competencies these learning processes are made visible, accredited and recognized to a different extent. And it can be expected that these differences are reflected in the destinations of the young people after leaving the projects:

- In the case of *Chapitô* young people when leaving the course obtain a qualification that formally is comparable to qualifications from conventional training. Those who complete their courses of training, at least have some hope that they can secure a job in their chosen area of performance. As an average, about 2/3 of the students from the Arts course who graduate pursue jobs in professional artistic productions (circus, theatre, TV etc.) or in social or community-based arts organizations. The others – due to the extended length and quality of training – have at least the possibility to try and use their skills for setting up an own circus or theatre company.

- In the case of *Hope Street* young people do not acquire a proper qualification comparable to that provided by Chapitô but at least they gain qualification credits which open them access to further education and training. So rather than qualifications for jobs Hope Street provides career opportunities. 60 per cent of those students who had finished the first Workshop Leaders course at Hope Street managed to secure a career in the arts or community sector. It appears that the New Deal has had a positive impact in this regard, despite the bad press it has received in Britain for its bureaucratic and sanctioning aspects. Due to the European Transitions-to-Work project it has even been possible for the organization itself to support some young people in making their careers more sustainable after the course.

- As far as *JUST* is concerned, its priority was to empower young people through the acquisition of important social skills and competencies. The achievements of the project were illustrated by the group's success in a local theatre festival for students and in its selection as a pilot project for 'a neighbourhood-based prevention of labour market exclusion' by the German Ministry for Labour. However, this project was the least vocational of the three and none of the participants in the drama group has directly qualified for a job. The involvement in the theatre group does not pay off for the participants in terms of qualifications or even a bonus with regard to later entrance into regular education and training. In the best case the young people succeed in translating their experiences, their increased self-confidence and their motivation into improving their school qualifications or into 'performing' well in interview situations. In the worst case they have to separate these experiences from the life perspectives and to split 'being oneself' from their careers.

Coming back to the question whether the potentials of informality are compatible with professional and organizational recognition we have to draw an ambiguous picture. On the one hand this tension seems to be manageable in the Portuguese and the UK contexts where the education systems are open enough to include arts-based courses. In effect, the informal provides a route in for young people that are at risk of exclusion. It encourages them that at least some aspects of formal education are compatible with their needs. These projects channel young people's creative energies. As Wenger argues,

> 'What does look promising are inventive ways of engaging students in meaningful practices, of providing access to resources that enhance their participation, of opening their horizons so they put themselves on learning trajectories they can identify with, and of involving them in actions, discussions, and reflections that make a difference to the communities that they value.' (Wenger 1998, p. 10)

On the other hand, in these contexts the price to be paid is that those young people who maybe need such informal approaches most urgently – because of their extremely negative experiences with school and other state institutions courses – are more and more excluded from the projects.

In contexts however like the German the rigidity of structures inhibits both the recognition of informal learning through formalization and the side-effects of such compromising.

Such projects cannot cure these problems steming from the implementation in a non-satisfying structural context of transitions. They remain political problems worthy of immediate attention. It is very important that we stress this point. Otherwise the unintentional implication would be that if such learning empowers young people, they will be liberated and motivated through a process of individualization. Political and social structures are such that this is not the case. Young people are, for example, still more likely to be affected by economic down-turn than any other social group. It might be suggested, albeit wrongly, that an evaluation of the three projects promote or support a liberalist view of the world in which the individual is all. In actual fact, they serve to highlight the deficiencies of European-wide training systems that so not provide the necessary foundations for young people's successful futures. They represent a deep critique of a system that does not encourage young people to feel that they belong to a social context of mutual recognition and support. These projects constitute more than simply a preparation for individualized transitions. As one young person we interviewed put it, 'this is not just a course, it takes over your life'. These programmes makes young people the authors of their own training. This in itself is more than an adequate indication of the limitations of European training programmes in general.

Chapter 6

Conclusions

This book started from an analysis of the changes youth as life phase is undergoing in a changing world. We have embedded the process of entering the labour market in wider biographical contexts and the societal developments which influence every single of these contexts – and above all, the way these contexts have to be inter-related in a biographically meaningful way by the young women and men themselves. We have argued that this process of biographization of youth is scarcely reflected especially by education and training policies but also by mainstream youth research which still are based on the assumption of youth as a status passage to a stable stage of adulthood with clear and reachable criteria – instead of acknowledging the ups and downs of the real transition process. We also have made the point that this is one of the reasons why there is a growing mistrust among young women and men towards societal institutions which can no longer keep their vague promises of social integration and still demand a lot of resources like motivation. Our starting hypotheses was that training and education offers to young people are likely to bridge this gap if they offer alternative ways of learning. Performing arts, according to us, should be especially apt to feature these new forms of learning. To find out to which extent and in which way these indirect forms of learning are happening, we have conducted three multi-facetted case studies on community-based education and training courses for young women and men who, for some reason or other, had disengaged with other forms of training. These courses in Lisbon, Portugal, Liverpool, United Kingdom, and Mannheim, Germany, offered training in performing arts such as music, drama and dance.

Our findings show that the courses in Lisbon, in Liverpool and Mannheim offered an educational setting in which learning is likely to be closely related to several aspects of identity work. Firstly, it provides the young women and men with a secure biographical space where they can develop self-confidence and self-consciousness. There seem to be several circumstances which make this probable: these courses offer their participants something valuable and socially recognized to do. Additionally, performing arts provide a good means to open up a stage where identity constructions

and perceptions of the self are easily accessible for reflection without as-
cribing personal and social learning deficits to the young people like many
mainstream schemes do. Identity and learning this way become a negotiated experience (cf. Wenger, 1998).

The projects we have evaluated as part of this research can be described
as models of 'good practice' which currently exist at the fringes and as such
could be spread into a much broader training landscape. We are not advo-
cating a single model of youth training here and do not mean to imply that
this is the only model that can be effective. Rather, we want to argue, that
this approach is especially effective in providing skills and competencies
related to coping with uncertain transitions. If policies follow the objective
to empower young people in a sustainable way such approaches are worth
extending. This can imply the awareness building in the framework of
training for teachers, youth workers but also artists and cultural producers.
This necessarily means an openness for specific financial support in setting
up new drama groups and clubs (which may not normally receive such
support simply because they are deemed 'unconventional' and not 'serious'
education) and arguably even, a re-assessment of the role of performance-
related subjects in mainstream education. In a more general sense this has
also to lead to a social process re-thinking of what learning and training are
about.

Secondly, the projects manage to bridge the gap between social and
symbolic aspects of youth lifestyles and the perception of youth prevailing
in education and training institutions. All three projects maintain close relationships to social communities, although the ones based in Liverpool and
Lisbon do not explicitly follow a neighbourhood-oriented approach, but
define community in the wider sense of local youth culture. The outcomes
of our evaluation show the benefits to be obtained if training is contextualized as far as possible both culturally and regionally or locally. The Hope
Street example illustrates that community links are important in two main
ways: they give participants the opportunity to do something which they
feel is important to the local community and which therefore has a wider
relevance than simply serving their own personal needs. They also give the
community the opportunity to direct its needs to the project, and to benefit
directly from these competencies and skills. These projects therefore provide a concrete opportunity for community collaboration: young people can
benefit from active membership in their community, and vice versa: local
institutions can directly verbalize and address their needs to such projects.
Ideally such links would open up access to jobs after the training programme.

The lesson to be learnt from these community-related experiences for both training and research is to explicitly include community links. Our research has clearly illustrated the benefits to be had from youth training that seeks to give something back to the community. A purely economistic model of training represents a short-sighted vision of what training can achieve. But the potential benefits of training will remain unrealized unless that training is envisaged as a two-way process. Contrary to many of the media generated visions of what motivates young people, our respondents were clearly enlivened by the opportunity to play an active role in dealing with some of the inequalities to which they themselves had been subjected. The community-focused nature of the training programmes evaluated not only had considerable benefits for the young people being trained, but also for the long-term futures of those communities. Our suggestion then is that youth training is most effective when approached holistically rather than simply instrumentally economic, and as a tool for encouraging both informal and formal links between training organizations, young people and the communities in which they grow up. Young people interact with their local communities. Training that encourages such interaction is more likely to encourage and motivate young people. Our research suggests that young people actively engage in their local communities – and even more so, if they are given the opportunity. This participatory impetus should be one of the primary issues of youth training. Organizations which offer training that has an active role to play in regenerating local communities should be encouraged and should attract investment. In this context, it may also be particularly beneficial to encourage the development of 'virtual professional communities'; networks of interested parties who can work together to construct a more coherent agenda for youth training.

A third factor for the success of this integration process was what we have characterized by the term 'informality': according to Kahane's definition of the term (cf. Kahane, 1997), the projects feature a set of properties – such as reciprocal relationships between trainers and participants, openness to experiential activities and a combination of activities performed for their own sake with those aiming at future goals – which are essential to successfully stipulate informal learning. Following immediately on from the above, there needs to be an explicit recognition that learning is very much distinguishable from teaching. This is one of the most striking conclusions to emerge from this study. These young people are able to learn, because they find themselves in an environment which motivates them to learn despite the fact they were more than deeply de-motivated before joining the course concerned. These courses offer them a stimulating atmosphere which proposes alternative ways of relating to fellow trainees and adults and which encourages them to develop their own interests. This training works because it takes place in a 'safe' place: a place in which young people feel they can belong and in which they feel their training can belong to them. These courses are successful because they adapt to young people's sense of self. From this point of view training cannot be designed to be an inevitable success, but it can be designed in such a way that enables young people to really take part and to make it their ownsuccess.. We therefore quote again Etienne Wenger:

> '*Learning cannot be designed*: it only can be designed *for* – that is, facilitated or frustrated.' (Wenger, 1998, p. 229)

There must be a more conscious recognition that the sorts of informal factors we have discussed during this book, factors which facilitate learning and provide motivation have an important part to play in the development of curricula. Training can be of genuine long term benefit if it allows young people to take an active part in their own learning. The courses do achieve this because they do not define young women and men as passive recipients of teaching. The factors which we have discussed help to create an atmosphere in which young people take on their own self-responsibility. However, this point is perhaps in more danger than any other, of being lost in a sea of rhetoric. It is a very easy point to make, but is more difficult to put into practice. Any training policy can superficially adopt such a philosophy, however, 'top-down' that training might be. The danger is that the onus on learning, simply provides an excuse to mask the inefficiencies of present training regimes. It, potentially at least, can actually act as a deterrent to radical change, insofar as it encourages minor alterations in existing training programmes rather than a complete overhaul of the system. The latter would be necessary to address the needs of those who want and need to be trained. The status quo appears to be such that young people often do not engage with the training they are given. It is not enough to say 'we need learning driven training regimes'. It is unlikely that young people invest more in their learning experience when that learning experience is, in actual fact, not one they want to have in the first place. In contrast, all case studies have confirmed the close relation between choice, identification and motivation.

In the courses we investigated during this project 'success' is defined in a more qualitative way than is generally the norm. The implication of this is that if young people are highly motivated by the training they receive they are more likely to overcome the stresses and strains associated with 'risky' transitions. In other words, transitions can be only be regarded as successful if they combine success in systemic terms of qualifications and jobs with subjective satisfaction. This key finding necessitates some structural changes which will vary on a national basis as a result of the differences between the respective transitional systems. Above all, however, transitional systems need to open themselves up to more innovative practice. In the case of Chapitô this has already, at least partly, been realized. The acknowledgement as an EPAOE trainign course can serve as a useful model for further structural innovations in the Portuguese training system. As far as Hope Street in Liverpool is concerned, initial fears of their training programme being 'colonized' by the New Deal have diminished. It could even be said that in some respect at least these broader national developments actually compliment the values that underlie the Hope Street project. In both cases, the on-going success for individual participants of the projects depend on the willingness of the labour market to accept such qualifications. Both projects try to do their best in opening up access to this labour market by establishing contacts during the training process. But the training-to-work-transition continues to be precarious in nature.

Also if one neglects the contextual differences and starts from conditions as in Portugal or the UK, the recognition of informal learning in order to empower young people in a sustainable way still poses a dilemma: the most important form of recognition is to include respective projects into the formal system. Up to now there are only two options:

• Either one accepts their peripherical situation for the sake of applying their principles without compromising as it is the case with JUST in Mannheim; there Boal's Theatre of the Oppressed is most visible. This means to accept limited funding and limited accreditation for the young people's careers as well.

• Or one opts for including informal learning into the formal system, a way which is pleaded for by many youth work organizations have chosen and for which the term 'non-formal education' has been coined (European Youth Forum 1999). Both Hope Street and Chapitô stand for this approach as they have introduced more standardized curricula leading to qualifications. And in both cases the effects of such a policy are visible: over the years the access thresholds have been raised in order to make sure that the young people in the course succeed in achieving the qualifications.

This dilemma could only be solved by new forms of recognition of informal learning; forms of assessment that address the individuals and relate to the skills, competencies and knowledge that they have acquired during their learning biographies. Such processes inevitably have to be symmetric communication processes in which the assessed persons share the definition (or evaluation) power with the assessors, in which the forms of demonstrating individual strengths are open to individual appropriateness and preference, in which individuals can perform their experiences (cf. CEDEFOP 1997; 1999). Under such conditions settings of informal learning could be recognized (and funded) without setting participants and professionals under pressure of producing measurable outcomes whilst individuals are liberated from being selected according to segmented education and training opportunities. It is clear that the acceptance of such forms of recognition imply fundamental changes of national transition systems. Not only would structures of selectivity and segmentation be perforated but also institutions that operate on the basis of 'educational plans' (Böhnisch *et al.* 2002) would need to be open for unpredictable learning outcomes.

This implies a shift in current policy as not only projects with transparent economic pay-offs, but much more the learning process itself and the communal and participatory experiences provided by this process, are worthy of funding. Our research has illustrated that youth training cannot only aim to produce immediate results but is a medium to long-term investment which has much more to be evaluated according to mid- and long-term learning processes. . The current state of youth training encourages a state of mind in which programmes should have measurable effects in terms of formal success criteria criticised above. Accountability in itself reveals to be not so much the problem as with regard to accountability in the framework of these systemic success criteria. This framework is a self-perpetuating system that reproduces the very inequalities, divisions and economic imbalances it purports to address. Further youth training policies therefore should be oriented towards a longitudinal perspective. A young person securing a placement in a workplace after having completed a training programme is not in itself a successful measure . The experiential nature of that placement and the impact of that placement on the individual's personal biography is far more important and within this, economical interests are in many respects parallel to those of young people themselves. This may require a leap of faith, but only when such a leap is taken will training provision be imaginative enough to occupy and stimulate the imaginations of young people themselves. In short, the rather static model of youth training that currently still exists needs to be superseded by a more flexible, reflexive, and pragmatic approach which actively embraces the sorts of innovations evident in the three training programmes we evaluated above (cf. Walther *et al.* 2002). Bona fide student-centred training programmes will produce their own economic pay-offs.

Alternative concepts of learning have to be given appropriate credence and should be integrated more effectively as part of a more rounded and coherent transition strategy. Of particular importance in this respect is the introduction of more open funding structures, which avoid fixed learning contents and curricula, and which actively encourage innovative approaches to training.

It has become obvious that re-thinking learning especially with regard to transitions between school and work implies re-thinking youth. Research plays the central role in this regard: the abiding legacy of this project is the richness of data which has self-consciously put young people's needs, priorities and meanings at the forefront of its agenda. This research project was what can be described as 'youth-sensitive'. It provided a forum in which young people were given a relaxed atmosphere in which they could discuss the pros and cons of their particular training 'biographies'. Although, in this context, it was important to recognize the impact on young people's lives of what are economically disadvantaged or highly demotivating conditions, the project set out not to valorize young people as 'victims'. Instead, this research was intended to address the complex nature of the structure-agency-relationship by looking at learning processes and how they can be enabled.

This research perspective is very much tied up with a longstanding debate concerned with the direction that youth research should be heading and in particular the apparent split that seems to have occurred between structural and cultural approaches to young people. As Miles (2000) notes, there exists a massive gulf between those researchers who focus on extreme cultural expressions of youth at one end of the spectrum and conceptions of 'disadvantaged' youth at the other. For a long time youth research has been related to institutional definitions of youth – either affirmatively by investigating in problems that youth had or made with regard to come to terms with institutionalized status passages or in neglecting the fact that those still are interlinked with young people's life-styles and symbolic production. The end result of this process is that generalizations about the nature of 'youth' continue to be made at opposite ends of the spectrum both actively and passively reproduce the normalizing institutional approaches. Most damagingly, bland discussions of youth 'transitions', based on broad trends in employment and education, actually serve to take young people out of the equation. In other words, young people are assumed to be victims and the active and creative ways in which they negotiate 'disadvantage' are almost entirely neglected,

'In this context, youth becomes little more than a term describing an undifferentiated mass of people of similar age experiencing similar things, when what it should be describing is a highly differentiated group of people of similar age subject to a whole variety of experiences depending upon a diverse range of personal experiences.' (Miles, 2000, p. 10)

Most lately the 'yo-yo-ization' of youth transitions (to which we have re-ferred in chapter 2) has liberated youth and young adulthood from a direct and output-oriented – in biographical terms – dependency relation from the status of adulthood. Youth increasingly has become a value of its own and increasingly young people have to be considered and respected as experts of their life-worlds. Understanding these means to enter into a symmetric communication process in which perspectives and definitions of both the researchers and the researched are equal. This is an issue taken up espe-cially effectively by Jeffs and Smith (1999) who are concerned with the implications of this problem for youth work. The core concern here, as Jeffs and Smith (1999) point out, is that far too much research pays little, if not no attention to people's actual experiences. In this context, we should reiterate that although each of the three projects have much in common, what they have most in common is an interest in giving young people a voice as a means of accessing the diverse opportunities we associated with a so-called 'risk society'. In short, this project is an example of the benefits to be had from research that takes account of the multiple spiralling nature of youth transitions and which does so in a flexible and reflexive manner. As Cohen and Ainley (2000) have argued, theoretical and practical consid-erations should be combined as part of a need to understand how young people 'learn' their way through everyday life. In short, according to Cohen and Ainley what we need to do is develop a theory of learning as cultural practice. As they argue,

'any kind of learning involves investment in personal meanings which in turn shape the sense of self. What is learnt is not just a skill but an identity, or rather a form of identity work. If you cannot manage the identity work entailed you will not manage to succeed in doing the activity. If you cannot see yourself as a budding chemist or rock musician then you are not going to get your head and your hands round a Bunsen burner or a guitar.' (Cohen and Ainley, 2000, p. 92)

Research that seeks to address the nature of young people's own meanings, what Cohen and Ainley describe as 'local situated knowledge' therefore represents a fundamental component of a reflexive youth research agenda.

Youth research will have to develop new innovative methodologies and projects that have young people's meanings at their core,

> 'Once we have this kind of local situated knowledge we may be in a better position to develop strategies of educational intervention and support that make sense to young people because they address their own narratives of aspirations and provide a meaningful supplement to the stories they tell themselves about the way their lives should go. How some young people learn to culturally labour more productively than others, why some are more able than others to turn their cultural labour into realizable forms of cultural capital, how this relates to 'social capital' formation and peer networks thus becomes the heart of the new youth policy research agenda.' (Cohen and Ainley, 2000, p. 93)

There is an important, indeed critical place, as this project has hopefully illustrated, for research which addresses the shared experiences manifested through young people's meanings, as opposed to simply tapping into what is little more than an assumed generational response (Jeffs and Smith, 2000). A particularly beneficial way of doing so might well be to promote investment in qualitative longitudinal research which is concerned with the meanings young people invest in their everyday lives (particularly in the context of youth training) and how those meanings are played out throughout the development of personal and career biographies. There is always the danger that youth research adopts an 'in-and-out' mentality in which the researcher takes a snapshot in time and generalizes from that snapshot. But it is the constantly changing nature of the 'youth' experience that such an approach may not be adequate. It may only be possible to come to terms with the ups and downs of youth experience and the implications of that experience for adulthood, if funders are prepared to invest in long-term research projects that look at the long term experience of so-called 'transitions' to adulthood and how the tensions and pressure associated with 'youth' are played out in later life. In short, as far as youth 'transitions' exist they form part of an on-going process of identity construction. Research should seek to both reflect and tap into this.

It is absolutely essential that the relationship between research, discourse and policy implementation is strengthened as part of a common strategy for action. In an understandable, but often misguided, effort to bridge the divide between theory and practice a lot of catch words have been developed which continue to be associated with youth research and policy. Concepts such as 'empowerment', 'participation' 'transferable skills', 'informal learning' and 'lifelong learning', which are often referred to with an only vague understanding what concretely is meant by them.

These concepts have to be concretized and contextualized to enfold their value for a general discussion. Above all, they have to be brought back to the concerning structural preconditions they would afford. Then they start to become really political concepts. Our discussion of the secondary learning effects in community arts' is an example for how these concepts may be contextualized and concretised in youth training that prioritizes young people's needs.

The potential here is enormous. The field of youth research has an incredibly complicated relationship with that of youth policy and the two fields do not always work in unison or, indeed, sing from the same hymn book. Inevitably, political and personal agendas not always have the empowerment of young people as a common goal. Empowerment is not, or at least, should not be a rhetorical notion. Rather, it relates to the diverse set of rights, responsibilities and power relationships in which young people partake. The development of youth training should be therefore very much a process of negotiation between youth research, policy makers and funders and, of course, young people themselves. Our final point then is this: If we recognize that 'youth' is experiential and is not simply a status passage then our training programmes and the way in which we monitor those programmes, need to reflect this richness of experience. Being a young person is very much about maximizing the moment and about feeling that you are fulfilling or 'finding' yourself in that moment. It is a qualitative and constantly changing experience and not a static one measurable by economic outputs. These outputs will only emerge if young people are allowed to develop appropriate skills in contexts which actively stimulate them. Ironically, an effective training programme is, in general, one that does not actually 'feel' like a training programme; one that simply gives young people the room in which they can start to find or be themselves. The challenge now is to take such a contention beyond the rhetorical stage and into the arena of practice and policy. Young people can only begin to find themselves if policy makers provide the foundations upon which they can do so. The three projects we have evaluated as part of this report illustrate the potential of what might be described as 'meaning-centred training'. Many of the young people we interviewed were brave enough to put themselves on the line when partaking in such training. The time has come for youth policy-makers and funders – as well as for researchers – to do the same.

Bibliography

Alheit, Peter (1995) Biographizität als Lernpotential: Konzeptionelle Überlegungen zum biographischen Ansatz in der Erwachsenenbildung in: H.-H. Krüger and W. Marotzki (eds) *Erziehungswissenschaftliche Biographieforschung*, Opladen: Leske and Budrich, pp. 276-307.

Alheit, Peter (1996) Changing Basic Rules of Biographical Construction: Modern Biographies at the End of the 20th Century in: A. Weymann and W. R. Heinz (eds) *Society and Biography*, Weinheim: Deutscher Studienverlag.

Allatt, Patricia and Yeandle, Susan (1992) *Youth Unemployment and the Family*, Voices of disordered times, London/New York: Routledge.

Almeida, João F., Pais, José M., Torres, Anália C., Machado, Fernando L., Ferreira, Paulo A. and Nunes, João S. (1996) *Jovens de Hoje e de Aqui*, Resultados do Inquérito à Juventude do Concelho de Loures, Loures: CMLoures Ed.

Antonovsky, Aaron (1987) *Unraveling the Mystery of Health*, San Francisco: Jossey-Bass.

Azevedo, Joaquim (1992) Portugal não é só um país de doutores (entrevista), *Revista Educação*, 5, pp. 5-12.

Azevedo, Joaquim (1999) Emprego e Integração no Mercado de Trabalho. Perspectivas de Política, *Sociedade e Trabalho*, 7, pp. 83-87.

Baethge, Martin (1999) Glanz und Elend des deutschen Korporatismus in der Berufsbildung, *WSI-Mitteilungen* 8/1999.

Banha, Rui B., Gaspar, Ana M., Gomes, Maria do Carmo, Miles, Steven and Pohl, Axel (1999) Catching the Trapeze in a Lifelong Learning Society: A Comparative Discussion of Unconventional Educational Strategies for 'Disadvantaged' Young People, in A. Walther and B. Stauber (eds), pp. 219-228.

Banks, Michael, Bates, Ian, Breakwell, Glynis, Bynner, John, Jamieson, Lynn and Roberts, Ken (1992) *Careers and Identities*, Milton Keynes: Open University Press.

Bauman, Zygmunt (1992) *Intimations of Postmodernity*, London: Routledge.

Bauman, Zygmunt (1995) *Life in Fragments*, London: Blackwell.

Beck, Ulrich (1992) *Risk Society*, London: Sage.

Behrens, Martina and Brown, Alan (1994) Finding jobs: institutional support and individual strategies, in K. Evans and W.R. Heinz (eds).

Bendit, René et al. (1999) *Youth and Housing in Germany and the European Union*, Data and Trends on Housing: Biographical, Social and Political Aspects, Opladen: Leske and Budrich.

Biggart, Andy and Furlong, Andy (2000) *Misleading Trajectories*, report for Great Britain, http://www.iris-egris.de/egris/tser/uk.pdf

BMBF (1999) *Berufsbildungsbericht 1999*, ed. by Bundesministerium für Bildung, Wissenschaft, Forschung und Technologie. Bonn.

Boal, Augusto (1979) *Theater der Unterdrückten*, Frankfurt a.M: Reclam.

Boal, Augusto (1982) *The Theatre of the Oppressed*, New York/London: Routledge.

Böhnisch, Lothar (1997) *Sozialpädagogik der Lebensalter: Eine Einführung*, Weinheim / München: Juventa.

Böhnisch, Lothar (1994) *Gespaltene Normalität*, Lebensbewältigung und Sozialpädagogik an den Grenzen der Wohlfahrtsgesellschaft, Weinheim/München: Juventa.

Böhnisch, Lothar and Winter, Reinhard (1993) *Männliche Sozialization*, Bewältigungsprobleme männlicher Geschlechtsidentität im Lebenslauf, Weinheim/München: Juventa.

Bois-Reymond, Manuela du (1995) The Role of Parents in the Transition Period of Young People, in Bois-Reymond, M. du / Diekstra, R. / Hurrelmann, K. / Peters, E. (eds) *Childhood and Youth in Germany and The Netherlands*, Transitions and Coping Strategies of Adolescents, Berlin/New York: de Gruyter, pp. 73-104.

Bois-Reymond, Manuela du (1998) 'I Don't Want to Commit Myself Yet': Young People's Life Concepts, *Journal of Youth Studies*, 1, 1, pp. 63-79.

Bois-Reymond, Manuela du and Walther, Andreas (1999) Learning between Want and Must: Contradictions of the Learning Society, in A. Walther and B. Stauber (eds) *Lifelong Learning in Europe*, Volume 2, Tübingen: Neuling, pp. 21-45.

Bourdieu, Pierre (1983) Ökonomisches Kapital, kulturelles Kapital, soziales Kapital, in R. Kreckel (ed.) *Soziale Ungleichheiten*, Soziale Welt, Sonderband 2, Göttingen.

Bourdieu, Pierre (1998) *Praktische Vernunft: zur Theorie des Handelns*, Frankfurt a.M.: Suhrkamp.

Bradley, Harriet (1996) *Fractured Identities: Changing Patterns of Inequality*, Cambridge: Cambridge University Press.

Braun, Frank (1996) *Lokale Politik gegen Jugendarbeitslosigkeit*, Arbeitsweltbezogene Jugendsozialarbeit, Band 1. Weinheim/München: Juventa.

Brinkley, Ian (1997) Underworked and underpaid, *Soundings*, 6, pp. 161-171.

Bundesanstalt für Arbeit (1999) *Arbeitsstatistik 1998*, Nürnberg.

Buzzi, Carlo, Cavalli, Alessandro and De Lillo, Antonio (eds) (1997) *Giovani verso il Duemila*, Quarto rapporto Iard sulla condizione giovanile in Italia, Bologna: Iard.

Bynner, John and Robert, Ken (1991) *Youth and Work*, Transitions to Employment in England and Germany, London and Bonn: Anglo-German Foundation.

Bynner, John and Chisholm, Lynne (1998) Comparative Youth Transition Research: Methods, Meanings, and Research Relations, *European Sociological Review*, 14, pp. 131-150.

Bynner, John, Chisholm, Lynne and Furlong, Andy (1997) *Youth, Citizenship and Social Change*, Ashgate, Aldershot.

Cavalli, Alessandro and Galland, Olivier (eds) (1993) *L'Allongement de la Jeunesse*, Arles: Actes du Sud.

Cavalli, Alessandro and Galland, Olivier (eds) (1995) *Youth in Europe*, London: Pinter.

CEDEFOP (1997) *Training for a Changing Society*, Luxemburg: Amt für offizielle Veröffentlichungen der Europäischen Gemeinschaften.

Clarke, John (1979) *Jugendkultur als Widerstand: Milieus, Rituale, Provokationen*, Frankfurt: Syndikat.

Clarke, John, Hall, Stuart, Jefferson, Tony and Roberts, Brian (1975) Subcultures, Cultures, and Class, in S. Hall and T. Jefferson (eds) *Resistance through Rituals: Youth Subcultures in Post-War Britain*, London: Hutchinson, pp. 9-74.

Coffield, Frank (1999a) *Breaking the Consensus*, Lifelong learning as social control, Inaugural speech, University of Newcastle.

Coffield, Frank (ed.) (1999b) *The necessity of informal learning*, Bristol: Polity Press.

Cohen, Phil and Ainley, Pat (2000) In the Country of the Blind?: Youth Studies and Cultural Studies in Britain, *Journal of Youth Studies*, 3, pp. 79-95.

Denzin, Norman (1989) *The Research Act*, Englewood Cliffs: Prentice Hall.

Dias, Mário Caldeira (1997) *Avaliação das Políticas de Emprego e Formação*, Lisboa: IEFP.

Durkheim, Emile (1915) *The Elementary Forms of the Religious Life*: A Study in Religious Sociology, New York: Macmillan.

EGRIS (European Group for Integrated Social Research) (2000) Misleading Trajectories. Transition Dilemmas of Young Adults in Europe, *Journal of Youth Studies*, 3, pp. 150-159.

European Commission (1997a) *Employment in Europe 1997*, Luxembourg: Office for Official Publications of the European Communities.

European Commission (1997b) *Schlüsselzahlen zum Bildungswesen in der Europäischen Union*, Luxemburg: Office for Official Publications of the European Communities.

European Commission (1997c): *Eurostat: Youth in the European Union – from Education to working life*, Luxembourg: Office for Official Publications of the European Commission.

European Youth Forum (1999) *Building Bridges for Learning*, The recognition and value of non-formal education in youth activity, Brussels: European Youth Forum.

Eurostat (2000) *Educating young Europeans. Similarities and differences between EU member states and the PHARE countries*. Statistics in Focus 14/2000. http://www.europa.eu.int/comm/eurostat.

Evans, Karen and Heinz, Walter R. (1994) *Becoming adults in England and Germany*, London: Anglo-German Foundation.

Figueiredo, Alexandra L., Silva, Catarina L. and Ferreira, Vitor S. (1999) *Jovens em Portugal: Análise Longitudinal de Fontes Estatísticas (1960-1997)*, Oeiras: Celta Editora.

Fornäs, Johan (1995) *Cultural Theory and Late Modernity*, London/Thousand Oaks/New Delhi: Sage.

Funk, Heide (1993) *Mädchen in ländlichen Regionen* – Theoretische und empirische Ergebnisse zur Modernisierung weiblicher Lebenslagen, Weinheim/München: Juventa.

Galuske, Michael 1993: *Das Orientierungsdilemma*, Jugendberufshilfe, sozialpädagogische Selbstvergewisserung und die modernisierte Arbeitsgesellschaft, Bielefeld: Böllert.

Gelder, Ken (1997) Introduction to Part Seven (Sounds, Styles and Embodied Politics), in Ken Gelder and Sarah Thornton (eds) *The Subcultures Reader*, London/New York: Routledge, pp. 373-379.

Giddens, Anthony (1984) *The Constitution of Society*, Outline of the Theory of Structuration, Cambridge: Polity Press.

Giddens, Anthony (1991) *Modernity and Self-Identity*: Self and Society in the Late Modern Age, Cambridge: Polity Press.

Goffman, Erving (1959) *The Presentation of Self in Everday Life*, New York.

Habermas, Jürgen (1981) *Theorie des kommunikativen Handelns*, Frankfurt: Suhrkamp.

Hagemann-White, Carol (1992) Berufsfindung und Lebensperspektive in der weiblichen Adoleszenz, in K. Flaake and V. King (eds) *Weibliche Adoleszenz*, Zur Sozialisation junger Frauen, Frankfurt a.M./New York.

Hagestad, Gunhild (1991) Trends and dilemmas in Life-Course Research, An international approach, in W.R. Heinz (ed.) *Theoretical Advances in Life-Course Research*, Weinheim: Dt. Studienverlag.

Haunert, Friedrich and Lang, Reinhard (1994) *Arbeit und Integration*, Zur Bedeutung von Arbeit in der Jugendsozialarbeit am Beispiel von Projekten freier Träger, Frankfurt a.M.

Hebdige, Dick (1983) 'Posing ... threats, striking ... poses: youth, surveillance and display, reprinted, in K. Gelder and S. Thornton (eds) (1997) *The Subcultures Reader*, London/New York: Routledge, pp. 393-405.

Heckhausen, Heinz (1989) *Motivation und Handeln*, Berlin/Heidelberg: Springer.

Helfferich, Cornelia (1994) *Jugend, Körper und Geschlecht*, Opladen: Leske and Budrich.

Hodder, Ian (1994) The Interpretation of Documents and Material Culture, in N. Denzin and Y. Lincoln (eds) *Handbook of Qualitative Research*, Thousand Oaks/London/New Delhi: Sage.

Hodkinson, Paul (2001) Reworking Subculture: Young People and Elective Affiliation of Substance, *Leisure Studies Newsletter*, March 2001.

Hollands, Robert (1990) *The Long Transition*, London: Routlege.

Holzkamp, Klaus (1993) *Lernen: Eine subjektwissenschaftliche Grundlegung*, Frankfurt a.M. / New York: Campus.

Jeffs, Tony and Smith, Mark, K. (1998) The problem of 'youth' for youth work, *Youth and Policy*, 62, pp. 45-66.

Jeffs, Tony and Smith, Mark K. (1999) *Informal Education*, Conversation, learning and democracy, Ticknall: Education Now.

Jugendwerk der Deutschen Shell (1997) *Jugend '97* – Zukunftsperspektiven, gesellschaftliches Engagement, politische Orientierungen, Opladen: Leske and Budrich.

Kahane, Reuben (1997) *The Origins of Postmodern Youth*, Informal Youth Movements in a Comparative Perspective, Berlin/New York: De Gruyter.

Keupp, Heiner (1997a) Empowerment, in D. Kreft and I. Mielenz (eds) *Wörterbuch Soziale Arbeit*, Weinheim/Basel: Beltz.

Keupp, Heiner (1997b) Diskursarena Identität, Lernprozesse in der Identitätsforschung, in H. Keupp and R. Höfer (eds) *Identitätsarbeit heute* – Klassische und aktuelle Perspektiven der Identitätsforschung, Frankfurt a.M.: Suhrkamp, pp. 11-39.

Kohn, Melvin L. (1996) Cross-National Research as an Analytical Strategy: American Sociological Association, 1987 Presidential Address, in A. Inkeles and M. Sasaki (eds) *Comparing Nations and Cultures*, Readings in a Cross Disciplinary perspective, Englewood Cliffs New Jersey: Prentice Hall, pp. 28-53.

Kvale, Steinar (1996) *InterViews*, An Introduction to Qualitative Research Interviewing. Thousand Oaks/London/New Delhi.

Leccardi, Carmen (1996) *Futuro breve*, Le giovani donne e il futuro, Torino.

Lüscher, Kurt (1997) Familienrhetorik, Familienwirklichkeit und Familienforschung, in Vaskovics, L. A. (ed.) *Familienleitbilder und Familienrealitäten*, Opladen: Leske and Budrich: pp. 50-67.

Maffesoli, Michel (1993) *The Shadow of Dionysus*, A Contribution to the Sociology of the Orgy, New York: State University of New York Press.

Manninen, Jyri (1998) Labour Market Training Strategies in a Late Modern Society, in A. Walther and B. Stauber (eds) *Lifelong Learning in Europe*, Volume 1, Tübingen: Neuling, pp. 75-85.

Miles, Steven (2000) *Youth Lifestyles in a Changing World*, Buckingham/Philadelphia: Open University Press.

Miles, Steven and Cliff, Dallas and Burr, Vivien (1998) 'Fitting In and Sticking Out': Consumption, Consumer Meanings and the Construction of Young People's Identities, *Journal of Youth Studies*, 1, pp. 81-91.

Millar, J. and Warman, A. (1996) *Family obligations in Europe*, London: Family Policy Studies Centre.

Ministério da Educação (1996) *Dinâmicas, Memórias e Projectos das Escolas Profissionais*, Porto: ME Edições.

Moniz, António B. and Kóvacs, Ilona (1997) *Evolução das Qualificações e das Estruturas de Formação em Portugal*, Lisboa: IEFP.

Morgan, David L. (1997) *Focus groups as qualitative research*, Thousand Oaks: Sage.

Müller, Hans-Ulrich (1996) Fragile Identitäten und offene Optionen. Lebensentwürfe junger Erwachsener in einer westdeutschen Großstadt, in A. Walther (ed.), pp. 122-141.

NAP (National Employment Action Plan) (1999) Published by the Federal Government of Germany, Bonn.

Neckel, Sighard (1991) *Status und Scham*, Zur symbolischen Reproduktion sozialer Ungleichheit, Frankfurt/New York: Campus.

Neuroth, Simone (1994) *Augusto Boals 'Theater der Unterdrückten' in der pädagogischen Praxis*, Weinheim: Deutscher Studienverlag.

Nuglisch, Ralf and Pfendtner, Petra (1998) *'Ach, wissen Sie, unter kommen sie immer ...'* Die Berufsfindung Jugendlicher in einer ländlichen Region. Eine lebensweltorientierte Regionalanalyse zum Übergang junger Frauen und Männer im Alb-Donau-Kreis. Universität Tübingen, unveröff. Diplomarbeit.

Oechsle, Mechthild and Geissler, Birgit (eds) (1998) *Die Ungleiche Gleichheit*, Junge Frauen und der Wandel im Geschlechterverhältnis, Opladen: Leske and Budrich.

Oyen, Else (ed.) (1990) *Comparative Methodology*, Theory and Practice in International Social Research, London: Sage.

Pais, José Machado (1995) *Culturas Juvenis*, Lisboa: Imprensa Nacional Casa Da Moeda.

Pais, José Machado (1996) Erwachsenwerden mit Rückfahrkarte? Übergänge, biographische Scheidewege und sozialer Wandel in Portugal, in A. Walther (ed.) *Junge Erwachsene in Europa*, Opladen: Leske and Budrich, pp. 75-92.

Pais, José M. (1997) Grupos Juvenis e Modelos de Comportamento em Relação à Escola e ao Trabalho: Resultados de Análises Factoriais, in Cabral, Manuel V. and Pais, José M. (eds) *Jovens Portugueses de Hoje*, Oeiras: Celta Editora, pp. 135-187.

Pais, José Machado (2000) Transitions and youth cultures: forms and performances, *International Social Science Journal*, LII, 2, pp. 219-232.

Paterson, Lindsay and Raffe, David (1995) 'Staying on in full-time education in Scotland', *Oxford Review of Education*, 21, pp. 3-23.

Patton, Michael Q. (1990) Qualitative evaluation and research methods, Newbury Park/London/New Delhi: Sage.

Paul-Kohlhoff, Angela (1998) Ist der Beruf out?, in GEW (Gewerkschaft für Erziehung und Wissenschaft) (ed.) *Zukunft der beruflichen Bildung*, Dokumentation des Expertensgesprächs. Frankfurt a.M.

Peters, Els and du Bois-Reymond, Manuela (1996) Zwischen Anpassung und Widerstand: Junge Frauen im Modernisierungsprozeß. Nachrichten aus den Niederlanden, in A. Walther (ed.) *Junge Erwachsene in Europa*, Opladen: Leske and Budrich, pp. 93-121.

Pohl, Axel (1997) *'Ich bin ja schließlich hier geboren'* – Lebensbewältigung junger Männer aus türkischen Einwandererfamilien im Übergang von der Schule in den Beruf. Universität Tübingen: unveröff. Diplomarbeit.

Pohl, Axel and Walther, Andreas (1998) Dropping out in secondary education in Germany, National Report, in IARD 1998 (ed.) *Dropping out in secondary education in Europe*, Milano: Iard.

Pohl, Axel and Schneider, Sabine (eds) (2000) *Sackgassen, Umleitungen, Überholspuren?* Ausgrenzungsrisiken und neue Perspektiven im Übergang in die Arbeit. Tübingen: Neuling.

Preiß, Dagmar and Schwarz, Anne and Wilser, Anja (1996) *Mädchen – Lust und Last der Pubertät*, Frankfurt: dipa.

Pugliese, Enrico (1993) *Sociologia della disoccupazione*, Bologna: Il Mulino.

Rappaport, Julian, Swift, Carolyn and Hess, Robert (1984) *Studies in Empowerment: Steps toward understanding and action*, New York.

Reich, Robert (1993) *Die neue Weltwirtschaft*, Das Ende der nationalen Ökonomie, Frankfurt a.M./Berlin.

Roberts, Kenneth (1995) *Youth and Employment in Modern Britain*, Oxford: Oxford University Press.

Roberts, Kenneth, Clark, Stan C. and Wallace, Claire (1994) Flexibility and Individualisation: A Comparison of Tranistions into Employment in England and Germany, in *Sociology* 1/1994.

Rommelspacher, Birgit (1992) *Mitmenschlichkeit und Unterwerfung*, Frankfurt a.M.: Suhrkamp.

Schäfer, Heiner (1997) Abgedrängt – Der Einfluß des Übergangssystems auf die Marginalisierungsprozesse junger Männer am Arbeitsmarkt, in H. Felber (ed.) *Berufliche Chancen für benachteiligte Jugendliche?* Orientierungen und Handlungsstrategien. Arbeitsweltbezogene Jugendsozialarbeit, Bd. 2. Weinheim/München: Juventa.

Scheuch, Erwin K. (1996) Theoretical Implications of Comparative Survey Research: Why the Wheel of Cross-Cultural Methodology Keeps on Being Reinvented, in A. Inkeles and M. Sasaki (eds) *Comparing Nations and Cultures*, Readings in a Cross-Disciplinary perspective, Englewood Cliffs: Prentice Hall, pp. 57-73.

Sennett, Richard (1998) *Der flexible Mensch*, Die Kultur des neuen Kapitalismus, Berlin: Springer.

Skelton, Tracey and Valentine, Gill (eds) (1998) *Cool places*, Geographies of youth cultures, London / New York: Routledge.

Smith, Richard J. and Maughan, Tim (1998): Youth Culture and the Making of the Post-Fordist Economy, Dance Music in Contemporary Britain, *Journal of Youth Studies*, 1, pp. 211-230.

Stake, Robert E. (1994) Case Studies, in N. Denzin and Y. Lincoln (eds) *Handbook of Qualitative Research*, London: Sage, pp. 236-247.

Statistisches Bundesamt (1999*) Bildung im Zahlenspiegel*, Wiesbaden.

Stauber, Barbara (1999) Starke Mädchen – Kein Problem?, *Beiträge zur feministischen Theorie und Praxis*, 22, 51, pp. 53-64.

Stauber, Barbara and Walther, Andreas (1999) *Institutionelle Risiken sozialer Ausgrenzung im deutschen Übergangssystem*, National report on Germany (West) for the thematic network 'Misleading Trajectories', Working Paper, Tübingen.

Stauber, Barbara and Walther, Andreas (eds) (1999) *Lifelong Learning in Europe*, Vol. 2: Differences and Divisions, Strategies for Social Integration and Individual Learning Biographies, Tübingen: Neuling.

Stroobants, Verle (1999) Women's Ways of Learning for Work: Learning and Work in Female Biographies, in A. Walther and B. Stauber (eds:) *Lifelong Learning in Europe*, Volume 2, Tübingen: Neuling, pp. 129-136.

Thiersch, Hans (1986) *Erfahrung der Wirklichkeit*, Weinheim and München: Juventa.

Van-Waterschoot, Lucy (1998) *Plymouth Youth Speaks*, Plymouth: Plymouth Community Safety Partnership.

Walther, Andreas (2000) *Spielräume im Übergang in die Arbeit*, Junge Erwachsene im Wandel der Arbeitsgesellschaft in Deutschland, Italien und Großbritannien, Weinheim/München: Juventa.

Walther, Andreas and Stauber, Barbara and Bolay, Eberhard and du Bois-Reymond, Manuela et al. (1999) New Trajectories of Young Adults in Europe. A Research Outline, in CYRCE – Circle for Youth Research Cooperation in Europe (ed.) *European Yearbook on Youth Policy and Research*, Volume 2: Intercultural Reconstruction, Berlin/New York: De Gruyter, pp. 61-87.

Wenger, Etienne (1998) *Communities of Practice*, Learning, Meaning and Identity, Cambridge: Cambridge University Press.

West, Candace and Zimerman, Don H. (1987) 'Doing Gender', *Gender and Society*, 1, 2, pp. 125-151.

Wilkinson, Clive (1995) *The Drop Out Society*: Young People on the Margin, London: Youth Work Press.

Zenke, Karl G. 1995: Der Zerfall der Hauptschulbildung, Über die Vergeblichkeit des Versuchs, einen 'volkstümlichen Bildungsgang zu modernisieren', *Die Deutsche Schule*, 3/1995.

Index

Acting Up 61, 66-72, 74-75, 110-112, 114
adulthood 9, 19, 121, 129
agency 19-23, 127
Alheit, P. 19, 21, 24, 51, 131
Allatt, P. and Yeandle, S. 9, 131
autonomy 7, 15, 16, 19, 93, 98, 104

Bauman, Z. 8, 21, 131
Beck, U. 131
belonging 17, 22, 72, 85, 98, 103, 116
biographicity 24, 98
biography 9, 16, 32, 51, 126
 - de-standardization 8, 9, 18, 101
 - fragmentation 8, 22, 101
Boal, A. 45, 46, 53, 104, 125, 132
body 73, 85, 105
Böhnisch, L. 16, 18, 19, 126, 132
Bois-Reymond, M. du 9, 14, 16, 19, 23, 35, 132, 136, 138
Bourdieu, P. 21, 132
Bynner, J. 57, 131, 132

Cavalli, A. and Galland, O. 7, 132, 133
Chapitô 3, 80-97, 102, 112, 118, 125
citizenship 8, 55
Clarke, J. 19, 133
Coffield, F. 4, 106, 133
Cohen, P. and Ainley, P. 7, 128, 129, 133
community 3, 5, 43, 45, 47, 54, 62, 64, 67, 69, 75, 95, 100, 102, 105, 106, 109-114, 116, 118, 121, 122-123, 130
community arts 2, 3, 130
community work 54, 67

comparison 30, 34-36, 97, 114
competencies 1, 3, 7, 10, 19, 23-24, 26-27, 51, 104, 109, 112-113, 117-118, 122, 125
 - social competencies 23, 118
coping strategies 8, 18, 23
culture 8, 14, 16, 20, 22, 50, 55, 56, 64, 75, 117
curriculum 2, 4, 48, 51, 69, 80-84, 98, 107, 108, 115

dance 3, 81, 83, 86, 90, 121
dependency 7, 15, 43, 56, 73, 128
de-standardized transition 9
disadvantaged 2, 11, 27, 41, 44, 55, 61, 69, 76, 95, 127
diversification 18
drama 2, 3, 32-33, 44-55, 61-65, 73, 97-98, 101-106, 111-112, 118, 121-122

education 1-3, 10-12, 18, 20, 25, 35, 38, 40, 42, 44, 45, 48, 51, 53, 54, 56, 57, 59, 61, 63, 67, 77, 78, 79, 81, 83, 84, 97, 101, 103, 104, 105, 108, 109, 111, 113-119, 121-122, 125-127, 133, 136
EGRIS 1, 12, 35, 133
employment 2, 10, 11, 12, 13, 14, 18, 23, 25, 37, 38, 40, 41, 42, 49, 53, 56, 57, 58, 59, 61, 68, 74, 78, 108, 114, 127
empowerment 4, 5, 23, 51, 104, 105, 116, 117, 129, 130
ethnicity 8, 16, 70, 116, 117
Europe vii, 1-2, 10-11, 14, 16, 37, 46, 60, 73, 104, 132, 133, 135, 136, 137, 138

- European Commission vii, 2, 11, 133
- European research *see* research
evaluation 5, 28-29, 32, 35, 97, 107, 109, 113, 120, 122, 126, 136
Evans, K. and Heinz, W. 18, 21, 131, 133
everyday life 1, 18, 25, 46, 70, 91, 92, 106, 128
experience 4, 13-14, 24-25, 28, 30, 32, 41, 53, 57, 58, 61-69, 71, 72, 76-77, 82, 86, 91, 92, 93, 94, 95, 98, 100-103, 105, 108, 115-116, 122, 124, 129, 130
experiment 24, 26, 50, 73, 105, 107
expressing oneself 50

family 8-9, 12-16, 19, 33, 44, 50, 51, 56, 77, 83-87, 89, 90, 95, 101, 107
finding oneself 97-99, 105
flexibility 3, 21, 83
focus groups 31
Fornäs, J. 17, 20, 21, 22, 133
fragmentation *see* biography

gender 3, 8, 9, 14, 15, 19, 37, 38, 59, 70, 94, 99, 116, 117
generation 13, 16, 54
Giddens, A. 23, 25, 98, 134
Goffman, E. 134
group dynamics 52, 90, 92

Habermas, J. 23, 134
Hagestad, G. 18, 134
Hebdige, D. 134
Helfferich, C. 20, 134
hidden curriculum 107
Hollands 134
Hope Street 3, 60-76, 105, 109-113, 118, 122, 125

identity 100, 122, 134, 138
- identity work 21, 22, 97, 121, 128

individualization 13, 18, 19, 22, 100, 119
inequality 9, 106
informal vii, 3-5, 12, 24, 26, 29, 41, 47, 61, 68, 91, 93, 97, 103, 106-109, 113-116, 119, 123-125, 129, 133
informal learning *see* learning
informality 107, 109, 113, 119, 123
institution 30
intergenerational relationship 8, 15, 16
interview 28, 30-33, 44-49, 64-67, 82-83, 90, 92- 94, 119

Jeffs, T. and Smith, M. 128, 129, 134
JUST 3, 43, 53, 54, 55, 97, 109, 110, 112, 113, 114, 118, 125

Kahane, R. 107, 123, 135
Keupp, H. 22, 135
knowledge 1-3, 19, 24, 29, 79, 109, 113, 125, 128, 129

labour market 1, 3, 8, 10-12, 14-15, 17-18, 37, 39, 44, 54, 57, 58, 59, 62, 77, 78, 101, 110, 114, 118, 121, 125
learning 1-3, 5, 7, 23-29, 31, 32, 33, 34-35, 41, 45, 48-51, 59, 68, 76, 80, 86-94, 97-109, 114-119, 121-128, 133-134
- direct learning 93, 103
- gender learning 99
- indirect learning 2, 5, 25, 93
- learning experience 27-28, 31-33, 48, 98, 108, 116, 124
- lifelong learning 3, 98, 129
- informal learning vii, 4, 5, 24, 29, 91, 93, 97, 103, 106-109, 114-116, 119, 123, 125, 129, 133
- peer learning 108
Leccardi, C. 16, 19, 135

life course 9, 19
life-phase 1, 9
lifestyle 8, 17, 61, 102
Lisbon 3, 32, 80, 81, 88, 110, 112, 121-122
Liverpool 3, 32, 60-63, 69, 110-112, 121-122, 125

Maffesoli, M. 135
Mannheim 3, 32, 43, 45, 53, 60, 110, 112, 121, 125
Manninen, J. 4, 24, 135
marginalization 10, 13
meaning 20, 22, 25, 27, 31, 33, 80, 101-102, 130
membership 48, 100, 116, 122
men 10, 19,, 44, 48, 51, 53, 57, 86
Miles, S. 17, 20, 31, 101, 127, 128, 131, 135
motivation 3, 5, 13, 20, 25, 41, 51, 58, 65, 97, 100-103, 106, 116, 119, 121, 124
music 2, 3, 44, 48, 61, 62, 81, 88, 111-112, 121

negotiation 8, 16, 46, 101-102, 130
neighbourhood 43, 44, 54, 88, 110, 112, 118, 122

Pais, J. M. 9, 21, 131, 136
peers 16, 50, 94, 101
performance 2, 5, 10, 21, 23-24, 29, 32-34, 46, 48, 53, 60-70, 73-74, 81-82, 85-86, 89-95, 99, 101-106, 112, 116, 118, 122
performing arts 3-5, 7, 24-26, 28, 45, 54, 61-62, 65, 67, 98, 103-109, 114-115, 121
practice 4, 14, 51, 65, 80, 100, 102, 105, 113, 122, 124-125, 128, 129, 130

qualification 11, 38, 39, 40, 42, 51, 63, 79, 102, 114, 118

research 1-5, 7, 10, 19, 22-23, 27-36, 48, 55, 58, 62, 67, 73, 89, 97, 103, 105, 122-123, 126-130, 135-136
- comparative research 35
- European research vii, 2, 11
- youth research 4, 5, 7, 21, 27, 35, 121, 127, 128, 129, 130
resources 4, 7, 9, 12, 18, 23, 80, 106, 116, 119, 121
risk 12-13, 15, 21-22, 37, 39, 42, 70, 86, 110, 119, 128
Roberts, K. 10, 11, 18, 58, 59, 131, 133, 137
role 3, 9, 13, 14, 15, 20, 24, 26, 30, 33, 38, 40, 41, 55, 58, 61, 77, 81, 84, 91, 94, 103, 106, 108, 112, 122, 123, 127
role model 9, 15

safe 26, 31, 52, 70, 104, 124
school 1-3, 7, 10- 12, 15-16, 37-40, 43-50, 52, 54, 56-58, 62-64, 79-88, 92, 94-95, 98, 108, 110-115, 119, 127
secondary learning effects 2, 49, 71, 130
self-confidence 2, 3, 5, 13, 26, 49, 94, 95, 98, 105, 119, 121
self-consciousness 98, 121
self-representation 21, 24
skills 1-3, 23, 28, 40, 46, 48-52, 58, 61-72, 75-76, 78, 80, 91, 94, 97-98, 100, 103, 106, 109, 110, 113, 115, 117-118, 122, 125, 129, 130
social policy 115
social resources 9
social skills 69, 112, 118
social work 40
sociology vii
space 7, 15, 23, 24, 28, 40, 65, 69, 94, 98, 99, 101, 115, 121
- safe space 31, 70, 104
- social space 17, 23, 102
status passages 1, 9, 127

Stauber, B. 4, 14, 16, 19, 131, 132,
    135, 137, 138
structure 5, 10, 17, 19, 25, 33-34,
    36, 38, 42, 43, 57, 82, 105, 113,
    127
style 17, 21, 24, 91, 103
sub-culture 20, 88

theatre work 104
training 1-3, 5, 8-13, 17-18, 20, 23,
    25, 26-35, 37-40, 42, 44, 48, 56-
    62, 64-67, 72-83, 86, 87, 91, 93-
    95, 97-104, 108, 110-127, 130
    - vocational training 11, 37, 38,
      39, 40, 43, 45, 54, 59, 79, 112,
      115
trajectory 94, 100, 116
transition 2, 5, 7-10, 12-13, 15, 17,
    19, 22-23, 27, 29, 35, 36, 37, 38,
    42, 57, 78, 94, 105, 115, 117, 118,
    121, 125-127
    - transition process 3, 13, 17, 22,
      121
    - transition system 5, 10, 23, 29,
      35, 36, 38, 42, 55, 57, 78, 114,
      118, 126

unemployment 1, 9, 10, 12, 15, 18,
    37, 39, 42, 43, 55, 56-58, 60-61,
    68, 77, 116

vocational training *see* training

Walther, A. 1, 4, 9, 21, 23, 30, 127,
    131, 132, 135, 136, 137, 138
Wenger 29, 100, 101, 102, 105, 119,
    122, 124, 138
women 44, 112, 137
work 10, 63, 64, 75, 93, 111, 118,
    132, 137

youth 2, 7, 10, 19
    - youth culture 8, 20, 21, 51, 63,
      122, 136, 137
    - youth policy 129, 130
    - youth training 29, 44, 57, 59,
      63, 65-66, 68, 76, 122-123,
      126, 129, 130
    - youth transition 4, 5, 7, 8, 22,
      27, 34, 37, 38, 41, 56, 128
    - youth unemployment 10, 37,
      41, 43, 58, 77, 78
youth work 2-3, 40-41, 43, 44, 58,
    112-114, 122, 125, 128, 134